THE WISDOM OF THE POPES

✦

A Collection of

Statements of

the Popes Since Peter

on a Variety of

Religious and Social Issues

◆

THE
WISDOM
OF THE
POPES

✦ ✦ ✦

THOMAS J. CRAUGHWELL

ST. MARTIN'S PRESS ➜ NEW YORK

THOMAS DUNNE BOOKS.
An imprint of St. Martin's Press.

Library of Congress Cataloging-in-Publication Data
Craughwell, Thomas J., 1956-
    The wisdom of the popes / Thomas J. Craughwell.—1st ed.
      p.   cm.
    Includes bibliographical references.
    ISBN 0-312-25356-7
    1. Catholic Church—Doctrines—Quotations, maxims, etc. 2. Popes—Quotations. 3. Quotations, English. I. Title.
    BX1751.2.C72   2000
    230'.2—dc21   99-089733

Designed by Carla Bolte

First Edition: April 2000

10 9 8 7 6 5 4 3 2 1

For Karen, Kathy, and John

✦

CONTENTS

✦

ACKNOWLEDGMENTS

✦

This book owes its origin to Greg Tobin, at the time, editor-in-chief of the Book-of-the-Month Club, who suggested that I collect some of the sayings of the popes. I owe a tremendous debt of gratitude to my agent, Jim Charlton, who believed in this project right from the start, and when I was bogged down defining obscure Greek theological terms, he gave me some great advice on how to structure my introductions.

I am especially grateful to Joseph Kung, president of the Cardinal Kung Foundation, for educating me on the state of the underground Roman Catholic Church in China.

My friends, Roger and Priscilla McCaffrey, have been tireless cheerleaders for this book, second only to my mom and dad, my sisters Karen and Kathy, and my brother-in-law, John Varda. My love and thanks to them all.

Finally, my profound thanks to Jim O'Halloran, librarian of the Maryknoll Seminary Library in Maryknoll, New York, and to Sister Regina Melican and the staff of the library at St. Joseph's Seminary in Yonkers, New York, for generously making their excellent collections available to me.

INTRODUCTION

✦

The popes are an unwieldy subject for any writer. There are so
many of them; they have reigned for nearly two thousand
years; and their influence, on history, politics, culture, and civilization throughout the world has been enormous. Every time I sat
down to write this introduction I found myself veering away from
the sayings of the popes and wandering off on other tangents.

So let me try to make one clear, simple statement about this
book now before I get off track again. It is not hard to find collections of papal documents in libraries, but it is almost impossible to
find any book that collects the most important, inspiring, and influential sayings of the popes in one volume. That is what I have
attempted to do in *The Wisdom of the Popes.*

While doing the research for this book I encountered some
extraordinary documents that are not papal writings but help the
reader understand a particular historical period or moral issue. In
the chapter on the popes and slavery, for example, I include
excerpts from a sermon St. Gregory of Nyssa preached against
slavery c. 385, a time when hardly a soul raised his voice against the
institution of slavery. In the chapter on the Mass, in addition to
reprinting in its entirety Pope Paul VI's 1969 address in which he
explained why he had taken the unprecedented step of rewriting
the text and rubrics of the Holy Sacrifice, I also included the letter
of protest written to Pope Paul two months earlier by two cardinals

who had grave reservations about the theology of the new Mass and the impact it would have on the spiritual life of the Catholic faithful. The chapter on the Church's struggle against communism includes excerpts from a document released in 1997 by the Donglai Township Committee of the Chinese Communist party instructing local party functionaries on what tactics they were to use to eradicate the "illegal" activities of the underground Catholic Church in China. My point in including this material is to underscore the fact that popes have been—and continue to be—major players in the great issues and events of the last two thousand years. Critics who assert that the papacy is a medieval relic out of place in the modern world have to contend with the considerable role Pope John Paul II played in the collapse of the Soviet empire.

I suggest that the papacy has been so influential in human history because it has endured longer than any other institution and outlived all its enemies. The Caesars, the barbarians, and the Arian heretics, the Holy Roman Emperors, the French Revolutionaries, and the Nazis—they are all gone, but there is still a pope in Rome. Any faithful Catholic can tell you the reason why.

Christ himself established the papacy when he declared that St. Peter was the rock upon which he would build his Church. To the apostle, Christ gave the keys to the kingdom of Heaven, promising that whatever Peter bound or loosed on earth would be bound or loosed in Heaven. The papacy, then, is a divine institution. Of course, the popes themselves are profoundly human, as frail and as fallen as the rest of us, which puts the pope in an unenviable position. He must build up and strengthen the Church. He must pass on intact the truths of the faith which Christ taught to St. Peter and the other apostles. He must be a shepherd to countless souls, doing all that he can to lead them away from sin and toward salvation. And he must accomplish all this while struggling against his own selfish, petty, and sinful impulses.

One could divide this selection of papal wisdom loosely into two categories: Faith and Morals. The first part shows the popes defining, defending, and confirming the essentials of Catholic doctrine. These essentials are generally known as the Deposit of the Faith, the complete collection of divine truths given by God to all people through the Holy Scripture and the traditions handed down from the apostles. It is the primary responsibility of the pope to safeguard these sacred truths.

Time and again, critics have demanded that the pope alter the content or the meaning of the faith to bring it into line with the trend du jour. Invariably they have predicted that the Church will become extinct if it does not accommodate itself to the prevailing philosophy. But if the popes possess any wisdom at all it is this: to hold fast to what is essential and eternal in Catholicism in spite of noisy dissent from within the Church or attacks—even bloody persecution—from forces outside it. We can see examples of this in our own day when Pope John Paul II is assailed continually by critics who demand that he change the Church's teaching on the sanctity of life, on marriage, on the priesthood, to bring the faith more in line with contemporary thought. At times, these howls of protest can be deafening. And there have been moments when it must have seemed as if the Church's opponents were invincible—for example, when Nero had St. Peter crucified, or Napoleon abducted Pope Pius VI and arrested his successor, Pius VII. It is reassuring to remember that Nero and Napoleon are gone, but the papacy is still here.

The second part of this book shows the popes exercising their moral authority by opposing slavery, the exploitation of workers, Nazism, communism, abortion, euthanasia, and assisted suicide. For many readers this part of the book may be the most interesting since it shows the popes wrestling with some of the most difficult moral issues of their time.

The case of Pope Pius XII and the Nazis is an interesting example since it reveals how perceptions of a pope can change over time. During World War II, both the fascists and the free world saw Pius XII as an implacable enemy of the Axis powers who worked to save the Jews of Europe from the Holocaust. More than fifty years later, Pius is routinely accused of being an anti-Semite, a do-nothing pope who sat in the splendor of the Vatican while millions went to their deaths, and a Nazi sympathizer who helped war criminals escape justice. Since the documentary evidence, including statements from Jewish leaders at the time, proves otherwise I am at a loss to explain why these calumnies against Pius XII continue to appear in books and newspapers.

Finally, I should say something about the popes as writers. Some wrote like angels. Others wrote like CEOs. St. Clement I, St. Gregory the Great, and St. Leo the Great were masters. Pope John Paul II often writes beautifully. And there is real fire in Leo XIII's landmark encyclical on workers' rights, *Rerum Novarum,* and Pius XI's condemnation of Nazism, *Mit brennender Sorge.*

Of course, this is only *a* book—not *the* book—of papal sayings. To read everything written by all 261 popes from St. Peter to John Paul II would be the labor of a lifetime. Because I could not be comprehensive, I have tried at least to offer selections that are representative of every era of the papacy.

Kingdoms and empires have passed away; peoples once renowned for their history and civilization have disappeared; time and again the nations, as though overwhelmed by the weight of years, have fallen asunder; while the Church, indefectible in her essence, united by ties indissoluble with her heavenly Spouse, is here today radiant with eternal youth, strong with the same primitive vigor with which she came from the Heart of Christ.

—St. Pius X, *Jucunda Sane*, March 12, 1904

THE WISDOM OF THE POPES

✦

WHO GOD IS

"No man hath seen, nor can see [God]," St. Paul writes in his first letter to St. Timothy. Nor has anyone been able to understand the ineffable mystery of God. "If you understood him," St. Augustine said, "it would not be God." Nonetheless, in every age believers have struggled to overcome the limitations of language and human understanding to express who God is, what God does, and what God's significance may be.

This much we know is true: God is eternal and living, without beginning and without end. God is one; there is no other. God is truth itself; he cannot deceive. By his wisdom, God orders and governs all creation. God is love, and his love endures forever. Through all our failings, through all our sins, through all our infidelities, God loves us still and waits for us to repent and ask for his mercy and forgiveness.

God is omnipotent, almighty. He created all things. He rules over all things. He can do all things. Since God is ineffable, his power is also mysterious. And because God is our Father, his power is loving.

It was out of love that God created the universe and made man in his own image. Humankind alone, of all the creatures fashioned by the hand of God, is able to know, love, and serve the Creator.

That God is one in three divine Persons—the Father, the Son, and the Holy Spirit—is the central mystery of the Christian faith. The Fourth Lateran Council in 1215 summarized the Catholic doctrine of the Holy Trinity as "three persons indeed, but one essence, substance or nature entirely simple."

The dogma of the Trinity asserts that the Father begets the Son; the Son is begotten by the Father; and the Holy Spirit proceeds from the Father and the Son. But these distinctions do not mean that one Person is less than another. The Son is equal to the Father, and the Holy Spirit is equal to the Father and the Son. Each of the three divine Persons is fully and entirely God.

The greatest minds of the Church—St. Augustine, St. Anselm of Canterbury, St. Thomas Aquinas—have attempted to explain the mystery of the Trinity. Yet the Triune God remains a mystery of faith in the strictest sense: the fullness of it is known and understood by God alone.

✦ ✦ ✦

God, raising up his Son, hath sent him to bless you; that every one may convert himself from his wickedness.

—St. Peter, Acts of the Apostles 3:26, c. 33

✦

The heavens, revolving under His government, are subject to Him in peace. Day and night run the course appointed by Him, in no way hindering each other. The sun and moon, with the companies of the stars, roll on in harmony according to His command, within their prescribed limits, and without any deviation.

—St. Clement I, *Letter to the Corinthians,* c. 95

✦

The fruitful earth, according to His will, brings forth food in abundance, at the proper seasons, for man and beast and all the living beings upon it, never hesitating, nor changing any of the ordinances which He has fixed. The unsearchable places of abysses, and the indescribable arrangements of the lower world, are restrained by the same laws.

—St. Clement I, *Letter to the Corinthians*, c. 95

✦

The vast unmeasurable sea, gathered together by His working into various basins, never passes beyond the bounds placed around it, but does as He has commanded.

—St. Clement I, *Letter to the Corinthians*, c. 95

✦

God desireth mercy rather than judgment.

—St. Anterus, Letter to the Bishops in the provinces of Boetica and Toletana, c. 235

✦

We must believe in God, the Father almighty; and in Christ Jesus, his Son; and in the Holy Spirit; and that the Word is united to the God of the Universe. "For," he says, "the Father and I are one," and "I am in the Father, and the Father in me."

—St. Dionysius, *Against the Sabellians*, c. 264

✦

In the Divine Trinity nothing is unlike or unequal, and all that can be thought concerning Its substance admits of no diversity either in power or glory or eternity.

—St. Leo I the Great, *Sermon 77*, c. 461

✦

Great and incomprehensible is the mystery of the Trinity. God the Father, God the Son, God the Holy Ghost, an undivided Trinity, and yet it is known because it is characteristic of the Father to generate the Son, characteristic of the Son of God to be born of the Father equal to the Father, characteristic of the Spirit to proceed from Father and Son in one substance of deity.

—Hormisdas, *Profession of Faith*, c. 520

✦

Though our lips can only stammer, we yet chant the high things of God.

St. Gregory I the Great, *Moralia on Job*, c. 604

✦

He is both above by virtue of His dominion, and beneath by virtue of His upholding; without, by His immensity, and within, by His subtlety; ruling from on high, holding together from below; encompassing without, penetrating within.

St. Gregory I the Great, *Morals,* c. 600

✦

We confess the holy and inseparable Trinity, that is, the Father, the Son and the Holy Ghost, to be of one deity, of one nature and substance or essence, so we will profess also that it has one natural will, power, operation, domination, majesty, potency, and glory.

St. Agatho I, Letter to the Third Council of Constantinople,
November 15, 680

✦

I adore You as my first beginning. I aspire after You as my last end. I give You thanks as my constant benefactor. I call upon You as my sovereign protector.

—Clement XI, *A Universal Prayer,* c. 1710

✦

God . . . can neither err nor deceive.

Pius IX, Qui Pluribus, 1846

✦

Magnify the Lord with me, We say in the words of St. Leo the Great, and let us exalt His name to one another; then We may praise God who is the source of all the graces and mercies We have received.

Pius IX, Beneficia Dei, June 4, 1871

✦

God is not only true, but Truth itself.

Leo XIII, Aeterni Patri, August 4, 1879

✦

God by grace resides in the just soul as in a temple, in a most intimate and peculiar manner. From this proceeds that union of affection by which the soul adheres most closely to God, more so than the friend is united to his most loving and beloved friend, and enjoys God in all fullness and sweetness.

Leo XIII, Divinum Illud, May 9, 1897

✦

Take away God, and all respect for civil laws, all regard for even the most necessary institutions disappears; justice is scouted; the very liberty that belongs to the law of nature is trodden underfoot; and men go so far as to destroy the very structure of the family, which is the first and firmest foundation of the social structure.

St. Pius X, Jucunda Sane, March 12, 1904

✦

Above all other reality there exists one supreme Being: God, the omnipotent Creator of all things, the all-wise and just Judge of all men.

Pius XI, Divini Redemptoris, March 19, 1937

✦

The truths that have to do with God and the relations between God and men, completely surpass the sensible order and demand self-surrender and self-abnegation in order to be put into practice and to influence practical life.

Pius XII, Humani Generis, August 12, 1950

✦

Whatever God has made shows forth His infinite wisdom, and it is manifested more clearly in the things which have greater perfection.

John XXIII, Pacem in Terris, April 11, 1963

✦

We believe that this only God is as absolutely one in His infinite Holy essence as in His other perfections: in His almighty power, His infinite knowledge, His providence, His will and His love.

Paul VI, Credo of the People of God, June 30, 1968

✦

These two names, Being and Love, express ineffably the same divine essence of Him who has wished to make Himself manifest to us.

Paul VI, Credo of the People of God, June 30, 1968

✦

God alone can give us right and full knowledge of Himself by revealing Himself as Father, Son and Holy Spirit, in whose eternal life we are by grace called to share, here on earth in the obscurity of faith and after death in eternal life.

Paul VI, *Credo of the People of God,* June 30, 1968

✦

If it is true that human life is in the hands of God, it is no less true that these are loving hands, like those of a mother who accepts, nurtures, and takes care of her child.

John Paul II, *Evangelium Vitae*, March 25, 1995

✦

In God's plan nothing happens by chance.

John Paul II, *Gift and Mystery,* 1996

II

JESUS CHRIST, TRUE GOD AND TRUE MAN

"The Son," says St. Ambrose, "is the Image of the invisible God." To reconcile sinful humankind to God the Father, God the Son came down from heaven and by the power of the Holy Spirit was conceived in the womb of the Blessed Virgin Mary and became man. The extraordinary event of the Second Person of the Holy Trinity taking on human flesh is called the Mystery of the Incarnation. Jesus Christ is truly God and truly man—two natures united in a single person. He is not some mixture of human and divine qualities, nor is he part God and part man. Jesus Christ had a human intellect and a human will, but they were subject to his divine intellect and his divine will.

Jesus Christ came into the world to reverse the damage wrought by our first parents when, tempted by Satan, they abandoned their trust in God, disobeyed him, and followed their own way in defiance of both God's love for them and his laws. The book of Genesis describes the moment when Adam and Eve lost their original innocence and holiness and were now corrupted by original sin: suddenly they were terrified of God, afraid of the natural world around them, even suspicious of one another.

In the Fall, the soul lost its control over the body; the harmony that existed between man and woman and between humankind and the rest of creation was shattered and sin and death entered the world. But even at this moment when it seemed that evil had overwhelmed the earth, God promised man a Savior. That promise was fulfilled in Jesus Christ, the Word made flesh.

As St. Gregory of Nyssa put it, "Sick, our nature demanded to be healed; fallen, to be raised up; dead, to rise again. We had lost the possession of the good; it was necessary for it to be given back to us. Closed in darkness, it was necessary to bring us the light; captives, we waited for a Savior; prisoners, help; slaves, a liberator."

By his death on the cross, Jesus Christ repaired the rift that had existed between heaven and earth since the Fall, atoned for the disobedience of our first parents by his perfect obedience to the will of the Father, and with his own blood ransomed the souls of all humankind.

Christ's resurrection confirms his divinity, gives authority to his teaching, and is the cornerstone of the Christian faith. As St. Paul put it, "And if Christ be not risen again, then is our preaching in vain and your faith is also vain" [1 Corinthians 15:14]. The resurrection of Christ brings God's grace to men once more and extends to us the promise of sharing the glory of eternal life in heaven.

Christ ascended into heaven, where he intercedes for us before the Father and sends us the gifts of the Holy Spirit. He reigns on earth through his Church until the Last Day, when he will return to judge the living and the dead and to establish a New Heaven and a New Earth. And although almost two thousand years have passed since Christ walked among us, his love for humankind has not diminished. For as it says in the Mass of the Sacred Heart, "The thoughts of his heart are to all generations."

✦ ✦ ✦

Thou art the Christ, the Son of the living God.

—St. Peter, Matthew 16:16, c. 30

✦

The Author of life you killed, whom God has raised from the dead, of which we are witnesses.

—St. Peter, Acts of the Apostles 3:15, c. 30

✦

Let us fix our gaze on the blood of Christ, and realize how precious it is to the Father, seeing that it was poured out for our salvation.

—St. Clement I, *Letter to the Corinthians*, c. 95

✦

Because of the love he had for us, Jesus Christ our Lord, in accordance with God's will, gave his blood for us, and his flesh for our flesh, and his life for our lives.

—St. Clement I, *Letter to the Corinthians*, c. 95

✦

I know one God only, Jesus Christ, and beside Him no other who was begotten and could suffer.

—St. Zephyrinus, c. 200

✦

The Wisdom, the Word, the Son of God took on human body, spirit and mind, that is, the whole Adam, or, to speak plainly, all our ancient humanity without sin.

—St. Damasus, Letter to Paulinus of Antioch, 375

✦

For just as by confessing that he assumed a human body, we do not thereby ascribe to him human passions and vices as well, so too by declaring that he assumed the spirit and mind of a man, we do not thereby assert that he suffered the sinfulness of human thoughts.

—St. Damasus, Letter to Paulinus of Antioch, 375

✦

Being perfect God, he became at the same time also perfect man, incarnate from the Virgin.

—St. Felix I, Letter to Maximus, Bishop of Alexandria, 431

✦

O the wonderful power of the Cross! O the unspeakable glory of the Passion!

—St. Leo I, *Sermon 59*, c. 450

✦

We could not overcome sin and the author of death, unless our nature had been assumed and made His own by Him Whom neither sin could stain nor death hold.

—St. Leo I the Great, Letter to Flavian, Bishop of Constantinople,
June 13, 449

✦

[Christ] spent Himself entirely to repair man who had been deceived, to conquer death and to destroy by His power the devil who held sway over death.

—St. Leo I the Great, Letter to Flavian, Bishop of Constantinople,
June 13, 449

✦

The true God, therefore, was born with the complete and perfect nature of a true man; he is complete in His nature and complete in ours.

—St. Leo I the Great, Letter to Flavian, Bishop of Constantinople,
June 13, 449

✦

Invisible in His nature, He became visible in ours; surpassing comprehension, He has wished to be comprehended; remaining prior to time, he began to exist in time.

—St. Leo I the Great, Letter to Flavian, Bishop of Constantinople,
June 13, 449

✦

For He who is truly God is the same who is also truly man . . . each of the two natures performs the functions proper to it . . . the one shines forth in miracles, the other is subjected to insults.

—St. Leo I the Great, Letter to Flavian, Bishop of Constantinople,
June 13, 449

✦

The very acts of Christ are precepts.

—St. Gregory I the Great, *Homilies on the Gospels,* c. 600

✦

The Redeemer imparted to the hearts of His disciples the Spirit who proceeds from Himself.

—St Gregory I the Great, *Moralia on Job*, c. 604

✦

He, the Maker and Redeemer of all men, who had he come in the majesty of his Godhead into the world, might have terrified mortals, preferred to descend through his inestimable clemency and humility to the estate of us whom he had created and thus to redeem us.

—St. Agatho I, Letter to the Third Council of Constantinople,
November 15, 680

✦

It is necessary to refer to him as God such things as are divine, and as man such things as are human; and each must be truly recognized through the hypostatic union of the one and the same our Lord Jesus Christ, which the most true decree of the Council of Chalcedon sets forth.

—St. Agatho I, Letter to the Third Council of Constantinople,
November 15, 680

✦

Immolated on the altar of the cross though He was innocent, [Christ] did not merely shed a drop of His blood—although this would have sufficed for the redemption of the whole human race . . . but a copious flood.

—Clement VI, *Unigenitus Dei Filius,* 1343

✦

There is in the Sacred Heart a symbol and a sensible image of the infinite love of Jesus Christ which moves us to love one another.

—Leo XIII, *Annum Sacrum,* May 25, 1899

✦

Men and states alike necessarily have their being from God through Jesus Christ, through whom every best and choicest gift has ever proceded and proceeds.

—Leo XIII, *Mirae Caritatis,* May 28, 1902

✦

It is altogether impossible to enumerate the heavenly gifts which devotion to the Sacred Heart of Jesus has poured out on the souls of the faithful, purifying them, offering them heavenly strength, rousing them to the attainment of all virtues.

—Pius XII, *Haurietis Aquas*, May 15, 1956

✦

Our Lord Jesus Christ by the sacrifice of the Cross redeemed us from original sin and all the personal sins committed by each one of us, so that the word of the apostle is verified: "Where sin increased, grace abounded all the more" [Romans 5:20].

—Paul VI, *Credo of the People of God*, June 30, 1968

✦

It is our sweet duty to honor and adore, in the Blessed Host, which our eyes see, the Incarnate Word Himself whom they cannot see.

—Paul VI, *Credo of the People of God*, June 30, 1968

✦

The Redeemer of man, Jesus Christ, is the center of the universe and of history.

—John Paul II, *Redemptor Hominis*, March 4, 1979

✦

In Jesus Christ the visible world which God created for man—the world that, when sin entered, was subjected to futility—recovers again its original link with the divine source of Wisdom and Love.

—John Paul II, *Redemptor Hominis*, March 4, 1979

✦

By His Incarnation, He, the Son of God, in a certain way united Himself with each man. He worked with human hands, He thought with a human mind. He acted with a human will, and with a human heart He loved. Born of the Virgin Mary, He has truly been made one of us, like to us in all things except sin.

—John Paul II, *Redemptor Hominis,* March 4, 1979

✦

The Lamb who was slain is alive, bearing the marks of his Passion in the splendor of the Resurrection.

—John Paul II, *Evangelium Vitae,* March 25, 1995

✦

"And the Word became flesh and dwelt among us." Such powerful words! They express the deepest reality of the greatest event ever to take place in human history.

—John Paul II, *Gift and Mystery*, 1996

III

THE HOLY SPIRIT

In the history of divine revelation, the Holy Spirit was the last Person of the Holy Trinity to be made known to us. St. Gregory of Nazianzen explained it this way: "The Old Testament proclaimed the Father clearly, but the Son more obscurely. The New Testament revealed the Son and gave us a glimpse of the divinity of the Spirit. Now the Spirit dwells among us and grants us a clearer vision of himself."

The Holy Spirit is a distinct person, yet is of the same substance as the Father and the Son, equal to them in glory and, like them, eternal. He proceeds from the Father and the Son, which is to say that the Holy Spirit is the gift of the Father and the Son to the world.

In some respects, the Holy Spirit remains the most mysterious Person of the Trinity. God the Father has spoken to humankind about himself. God the Son certainly has spoken of himself to us. But God the Holy Spirit, although he has spoken through the prophets, has never directly addressed humankind.

How then is the Holy Spirit known? In the life of the Church. He inspires the Scriptures. He supports the Church's teaching authority and he preserves its sacred traditions. He brings the faithful to communion with Christ in the Mass most particularly, but also in all prayer. And he manifests himself through the ministry of the Church and through the faith and good works of the saints.

The Holy Spirit's role in the salvation of man is impossible to underestimate. It was he who conceived the Son in the womb of the Blessed Virgin Mary and thus made Christ manifest to the world.

After Christ ascended into heaven, he sent the Holy Spirit to strengthen his Church and make it holy, a function the Holy Spirit continues to perform. Furthermore, it is the Holy Spirit who moves men to seek the truth, draws them to the Word of God, and opens their hearts and minds to receive the faith. "Through the Holy Spirit," St. Basil says, "we are restored to paradise, led back to the Kingdom of heaven . . . and given a share in eternal glory."

✦ ✦ ✦

Human sight can no more perceive the Holy Ghost than it can the Father or the Son.

—St. Leo I the Great, *Sermon 77*, c. 461

✦

Come, Thou Holy Spirit, come,
And from Thy celestial home
Shed a ray of light divine.

Come, Thou Father of the poor,
Come, Thou source of all our store,
Come, within our bosoms shine.

—Innocent III, *Veni Sancte Spiritus,* c. 1210

✦

[The Holy Spirit] would complete, in His office of Intercessor, Consoler, and Teacher, the work which Christ Himself had begun in His mortal life.

—Leo XIII, *Divinum Illud,* May 9, 1897

✦

For He who is the Spirit of Truth, inasmuch as He proceedeth both from the Father, who is the eternally True, and from the Son, who is the substantial Truth, receiveth from each both His essence and the fullness of all truth.

—Leo XIII, *Divinum Illud,* May 9, 1897

✦

As Christ is the Head of the Church, so is the Holy Spirit her soul.

—Leo XIII, *Divinum Illud,* May 9, 1897

✦

The Holy Spirit, the Comforter . . . bestowed the Scriptures on the human race for their instruction in Divine things.

—Benedict XV, *Spiritus Paraclitus,* September 15, 1920

✦

He [the Holy Spirit] enlightens, vivifies, protects and guides the Church; He purifies her members if they do not refuse His grace.

—Paul VI, *Credo of the People of God,* June 30, 1968

✦

We are called anew by the ever ancient and ever new faith of the Church, to draw near to the Holy Spirit as the giver of life.

—John Paul II, *Dominum et Vivificantem,* May 18, 1986

✦

Blasphemy against the Holy Spirit, then, is the sin committed by the person who claims to have a "right" to persist in evil—in any sin at all—and who thus rejects Redemption.

—John Paul II, *Dominum et Vivificantem,* May 18, 1986

✦

Even as we pray for the Spirit to come among us, he is already here.

—John Paul II, Homily in Central Park, New York City, October 7, 1995

✦

Just as in the Mass the Holy Spirit brings about the transubstantiation of the bread and wine into the Body and Blood of Christ, so also in the Sacrament of Holy Orders he effects the priestly or episcopal consecration.

—John Paul II, *Gift and Mystery*, 1996

IV

THE BLESSED VIRGIN MARY

"Centuries might pass," John Henry Newman wrote, "without formal expression of a truth which had been all along the secret life of millions of souls." Cardinal Newman's statement on how doctrine develops over time is especially true when one looks at the teachings about the Blessed Virgin Mary.

We'll begin with the two most ancient Marian doctrines: Mary's title, "Mother of God," and the special grace by which she conceived Christ without loss of her virginity and remained a virgin even after she had given birth to the Lord. These teachings can be traced back to the Age of the Apostles, particularly in the writings of St. Ignatius of Antioch (c. 37–c. 107), who was a disciple of St. John, the Apostle and Evangelist. Yet in spite of the antiquity of these teachings, controversies about them sprang up in the early centuries of Christianity. To settle the disputes, the popes, in conjunction with the first Church Councils, defined these two doctrines formally.

That Mary is truly Mother of God was defined at the Council of Ephesus in 431. Eyewitnesses reported that when the doctrine was announced to the crowd that had assembled outside the church where the council was meeting, the people began to chant over and over, "Holy Mary, Mother of God!"—an acclamation that Christians have repeated every day ever since.

Faith in Mary's perpetual virginity also goes back to the earliest years of the Church, yet it was not defined formally until the First Lateran Council in 649. Nonetheless, popes had defended the doctrine centuries before the council convened. In 390, Pope St. Siricius wrote to Anysius, Bishop of Thessalonica, to commend him for defending the doctrine that Mary was truly ever-virgin.

It is around this time that we begin to find written evidence regarding two additional Marian doctrines that certainly had become part of "the secret life of millions of souls": Mary's Immaculate Conception and Mary's Assumption.

"Immaculate Conception" means that from the first moment Mary was conceived in the womb of her mother, St. Anne, she was free from original sin. Just after the close of the Apostolic Age, the three greatest teachers of second-century Christianity were writing of Mary's sinlessness: St. Justin Martyr (100–167), St. Irenaeus (130–202), and Tertullian (160–240). The clearest, most direct, and most concise summary of Mary's Immaculate Conception comes from one of the greatest poets of the early Church, St. Ephrem of Syria (died 373). In a hymn addressed to Christ, St. Ephrem wrote: "Thou and Thy Mother are alone in this: you are wholly beautiful in every respect. There is in Thee, Lord, no stain, nor any spot in Thy Mother."

In spite of this ancient faith in Mary's freedom from original sin, debate and argument (some of it quite heated) raged around this point for centuries. St. Bernard (1090–1153), St. Albert the Great (1206–1280), St. Thomas Aquinas (1225–1274), and St. Bonaventure (1217–1274)—each renowned for his devotion to the Blessed Virgin—had qualms about the Immaculate Conception. To put it briefly, opponents argued that an immaculate conception, even of the Mother of God, suggested that Christ's Redemption was not universal, that Mary did not need to be saved. Blessed John Duns Scotus (c. 1265–1308) replied that, just like everyone else, Mary had been saved from sin solely by the merits of Christ. But because of her unique status as "full of grace," Mary was redeemed before she had any contact whatsoever with sin.

The issue was settled by Pius IX in 1857. He declared it a truth divinely revealed that from the moment of her conception, Mary was free from every trace of original stain.

Faith in Mary's Assumption is also very ancient. "Assumption" means that at the end of her life on earth, Mary was taken up to heaven, body and soul. The earliest surviving reference to the possibility of Mary's Assumption comes from St. Epiphanius, Bishop of Constantia in Cyprus. Around 390, he wrote, "Whether she died or was buried we know not."

At around this same time, August 15—the day still kept as the Feast of Mary's Assumption—was being celebrated in the East as the day of Mary's entrance into heaven. We know that by the year 650, the feast was being celebrated in the West. Pope St. Sergius I (reigned 687–701) decreed that August 15 should be one of the three feast days of Our Lady (the others being her Annunciation on March 25 and her Nativity on September 8), celebrated with a solemn procession to Rome's Basilica of St. Mary Major.

The Assumption was disputed in the universities during the Middle Ages, but this time St. Bernard, St. Albert, St. Thomas Aquinas, and St. Bonaventure joined with Blessed John Duns Scotus in supporting the doctrine. Pope Innocent IV (reigned 1243–1254) took a middle road: since the Church had not spoken definitively on this point, he said that the faithful were free to believe or not to believe in the Assumption of the Blessed Virgin.

It was Pius XII who in 1950 solemnly declared that Mary's

Assumption into heaven, body and soul, was a truth revealed by God.

It is only natural to ask if the popes, out of a misguided desire to honor the Blessed Virgin, are adding "new" dogmas that would have been unknown to the apostles. The short answer is "No." As Pius XI said, "The Church never adds anything to the sum of truths which are contained at least implicitly in the revealed deposit which it has received from God."

Pius XI's "revealed deposit," refers to what theologians call the "Deposit of Faith." Simply put, this deposit is the complete collection of divine truths given by God to all people through the Holy Scripture and the traditions handed down from the apostles. When the last of Christ's apostles died, the deposit was, for lack of a better term, closed. Everything that God intended for the Church to know was now known; nothing more could be added.

The deposit never changes. The Church, on the other hand, as a living, dynamic thing, does make progress in understanding the deposit of faith it has received from God. Time and again the popes have recognized as part of divine revelation truths that may have been only dimly perceived in the early years of the Church.

In the case of the Blessed Virgin, all the doctrines concerning her are firmly rooted in a text from St. Luke's Gospel. The Angel Gabriel addressed Mary as "full of grace," and ever since, the Church has been laboring to understand all that that greeting implies.

What can I say of her whom earth and heaven cease not to praise, though never as her merits deserve? May you believe beyond all doubt that, as she is higher and better and more holy than all human mothers, so she is more gracious and tender toward every sinner who turns to her. Cease, therefore, every sinful desire and, prostrate before her, pour out your tears from an humble and contrite heart. You will find her, I surely promise you, more ready than any earthly mother and more lenient in her love for you.

—St. Gregory VII to Matilda, Countess of Tuscany, February 16, 1074

✦

Almighty God enriched the Blessed Virgin with the gifts of His grace more abundantly than He enriched any other creature. He chose her from all mankind and at the word of an angel elevated her to the ineffable dignity of Mother of God. He adorned her with more radiance of glory than any other work of His hands.

—Benedict XIV, *Gloriosae Dominae,* September 27, 1748

✦

When she approaches her divine Son's throne, as advocate she begs, as handmaid she prays, but as Mother she commands.

—Pius VII, *Tanto studio,* February 19, 1805

✦

She is the best of Mothers, our safest confidant and in fact the very motive of our hope: she obtains all she asks for and her prayer is always heard.

—Pius IX, *Exultavit cor Nostrum,* November 21, 1851

✦

Nobody knows and comprehends so well as she everything that concerns us: what help we need in life; what dangers, public and private, threaten our welfare; what difficulties and evils surround us; above all, how fierce is the fight we wage with the ruthless enemies of our salvation. In these and in all other troubles of life, her power is most far-reaching.

—Leo XIII, *Magnae Dei Matris,* September 8, 1892

✦

In Mary, God has given us the most zealous guardian of Christian unity. There are, of course, more ways than one to win her protection by prayer but, as for us, we think that the best and most effective way to her favor lies in her Rosary.

—Leo XIII, *Adiutricem populi,* September 5, 1895

✦

The mightiest helper of the Christian people, and the most merciful, is the Virgin Mother of God. How fitting it is to accord her honor ever increasing in splendor.

—Leo XIII, *Adiutricem populi,* September 5, 1895

✦

When man has hardened his heart and hate has overrun the earth, when fire and sword convulse the world and make it resound with clash of arms and of wailing, when human plans have proved misleading, and when all social well-being is upset, faith and history point to Mary as the only refuge.

—Benedict XV, To the Consistory of Cardinals and Bishops, December 24, 1915

✦

Reign over men's minds, that they may seek only what is true; over their wills, that they may follow solely what is good; over their hearts, that they may love nothing but what you yourself love.

—Pius XII, *Exercise of the Royalty of Mary*, November 1, 1954

✦

Nothing seems more appropriate and valuable to us than to have the prayers of the whole Christian family rise to the Mother of God, who is invoked as the Queen of Peace, begging her to pour forth abundant gifts of her maternal goodness in the midst of so many great trials and hardships.

—Paul VI, *Christi Matri,* September 15, 1966

✦

Yes, Mary does bring us closer to Christ; she does lead us to him, provided that we live her mystery in Christ.

—John Paul II, *Gift and Mystery,* 1996

Mother of God and Ever Virgin

As regards the incarnation of the Logos . . . we believe in our Lord Jesus Christ, born of the Virgin Mary, who is Himself the Eternal Son and Word of God.

—St. Felix I, Letter to Maximus of Alexandria, 270

✦

You had good reason to be horrified at the thought that another birth might issue from the same virginal womb from which Christ was born according to the flesh. For the Lord Jesus would never have chosen to be born of a virgin if He had ever judged that she would be so incontinent as to contaminate with the seed of human intercourse the birthplace of the Lord's body, that court of the Eternal King.

—St. Siricius, Letter to Anysius, Bishop of Thessalonica, 390

✦

The Virgin gave birth to God by the power of Him who is possessed of all power.

—St. Celestine I, To the Synod of Bishops at Rome, 430

✦

We could not overcome the author of sin and death had not Christ taken on our nature and made it His. . . . He was truly conceived of the Holy Spirit within the womb of His Virgin Mother, who bore Him while preserving her virginity just as, preserving her virginity she conceived Him.

—St. Leo I the Great, Letter to Flavian, Bishop of Constantinople,
June 13, 449

✦

Mary, the mother of our Christ, ever a virgin, ought properly and truly to be called the God-bearer and the Mother of God the Word.

—John II, Letter to the Senators of Constantinople, 534

✦

Christ the Word was incarnate of the Holy Mother of God and ever-virgin Mary, and was made man.

—Vigilius I, Letter to Patriarch Eutychius of Constantinople,
December 6, 553

✦

If anyone does not, in accord with the Holy Fathers, acknowledge the holy and ever-virgin and Immaculate Mary as truly the Mother of God, inasmuch as she, in the fullness of time, and without seed, conceived by the Holy Spirit God the Word Himself, who before all time was born of God the Father, and without loss of integrity brought Him forth, and after His birth preserved her virginity inviolate, let him be condemned.

—St. Martin I, To the First Lateran Council, 649

Immaculate Conception

When, with that deep insight that comes of devout contemplation, we search and discover the sublime proofs of those merits which cause the Queen of Heaven, the glorious Virgin Mother of God, raised upon her heavenly throne, to outshine like the morning star all other constellations. . . . We deem it fitting, and even our duty, to invite . . . all the faithful of Christ to offer thanks and praise to God . . . for the wondrous Conception of this same Immaculate Virgin.

—Sixtus IV, *Cum praecelsa,* February 27, 1477

✦

Ancient is the piety of the Christian faithful toward our Blessed Mother, the Virgin Mary. They believe that her soul, in the first moment of creation and infusion into her body, was, by a special grace and privilege of God, and in consideration of the merits of Jesus Christ her Son, the Redeemer of the human race, preserved free from the stain of original sin. And it is in this sense that the faithful cherish and celebrate with solemn rites the feast of her Conception.

—Alexander VII, *Sollicitudo,* December 8, 1661

✦

Far above all the angels and all the saints so wondrously did God endow her with the abundance of all heavenly gifts poured from the treasury of His divinity that this Mother, ever absolutely free of all stain of sin, all fair and perfect, would possess that fullness of holy innocence and sanctity than which, under God, one cannot even imagine anything greater, and which, outside of God, no mind can succeed in comprehending fully.

. . . All our hope do we repose in the most blessed Virgin—in the fair and immaculate one who has crushed the poisonous head of the most cruel serpent and brought salvation to the world; in her who is the glory of the prophets and Apostles, the honor of the martyrs, the crown and joy of all the saints; in her who is the safest refuge and the most trustworthy helper of all who are in danger.

. . . Accordingly, by the inspiration of the Holy Spirit, for the honor of the Holy and undivided Trinity, for the glory and adornment of the Virgin Mother of God, for the exaltation of the Catholic Faith, and for the furtherance of the Catholic religion, by the authority of Jesus Christ our Lord, of the Blessed Apostles Peter and Paul, and by our own: We declare, pronounce and define that the doctrine which holds that the most Blessed Virgin Mary, in the first instance of her Conception, by a singular grace and privilege granted by Almighty God, in view of the merits of Jesus Christ, the Savior of the human race, was preserved free from all stain of original sin, is a doctrine revealed by God and therefore to be believed firmly and constantly by all the faithful."

—Pius IX, *Ineffabilis Deus*, December 8, 1854

The Assumption

This is she of whom the Holy Scriptures sing: the woman clothed with the sun, having the moon under her feet, and wearing a crown of twelve stars. This is she who bore in her chaste womb the Creator of Heaven and Earth. She alone crushes all heresies. She stands before the King who reigns in light, pleading for the Christian people as their bold advocate and most vigilant intercessor.

—Boniface IX, *Superni benignitas,* November 9, 1390

✦

We behold her taken up from this valley of tears into the heavenly Jerusalem, amid choirs of angels. And we honor her, glorified above all the saints, crowned with stars by her Divine Son, and seated at His side, the sovereign Queen of the universe.

—Leo XIII, *Jucunda semper,* 1894

✦

According to the general rule, God does not will to grant to the just the full effect of the victory over death until the end of time has come. And so it is that even the bodies of the just are corrupted after death, and only on the last day will they be joined, each to its own glorious soul.

. . . Now, God has willed that the Blessed Virgin Mary should be exempted from this general rule. She, by an entirely unique privilege, completely overcame sin by her Immaculate Conception, and as a result she was not subject to the law of remaining in the corruption of the grave, and she did not have to wait until the end of time for the redemption of her body.

. . . The revered Mother of God, from all eternity joined in a hidden way with Jesus Christ in one and the same decree of predestination, immaculate in her conception, a most perfect virgin in her divine motherhood, the noble associate of the divine Redeemer who has won a complete triumph over sin and its consequences, finally obtained, as the supreme culmination of her privileges, that she should be preserved free from the corruption of the tomb and that, like her own Son, having overcome death, she might be taken up body and soul to the glory of heaven where, as Queen, she sits in splendor at the right hand of her Son, the immortal King of the Ages.

—Pius XII, *Munificentissimus Deus,* November 1, 1950

V

IN PRAISE OF THE SAINTS

W hoever is saved is a saint. Consequently, every soul in
heaven is a saint. All the souls in purgatory are saints as
well because their salvation is assured. Yet the Church has always
felt impelled to pay particular honor to men, women, and children
whose lives and deaths could serve as models for all other Christians.

The earliest record we have of a pope formally declaring some-
one a saint dates from 993, when Pope John XV canonized Ulrich,
Bishop of Augsburg. The popes did not reserve exclusively to them-
selves the right to canonize until 1234. Today, "making saints," as
Kenneth L. Woodward calls it, remains entirely the province of the
Holy See, where the Vatican's Congregation for the Causes of
Saints sifts the lives of candidates to determine if they are worthy of
public veneration.

Long before the Congregation was created, even before Pope
John XV presided over Bishop Ulrich's canonization, saints were
being made by popular acclaim. Their names and stories were
recalled and retold by their neighbors at first, and then recorded in
local church calendars. Of the perhaps twenty thousand named in
the various martyrologies and other collections of saints' lives, the
majority have never had a formal canonization ceremony in Rome.
This is true of all the Apostles, of St. Joseph the husband of the
Blessed Virgin, of Mary's parents Sts. Anne and Joachim, of St.

John the Baptist, as well as such universally popular saints as St. George, St. Agnes, and St. Christopher.

For most of the twentieth century, Pope Pius XII was considered the most active in making saints. During his nineteen-year reign, he beatified twenty-three and canonized thirty-three individuals. His record has been surpassed, however, by Pope John Paul II. By 1999, he had raised 798 Servants of God to the rank of "Blessed" and declared 280 Blesseds to be "Saints."

✦ ✦ ✦

Paul demonstrated how to win the prize of patient endurance.

—St. Clement I, *Letter to the Corinthians,* c. 95

✦

This place, you should know, was once the abode of saints;
Their names, you may learn, were Peter and likewise Paul . . .
For Christ's sake and the merits of His blood they followed Him among the stars
And sought the realms of heaven and the kingdoms of the right eous.

—St. Damasus, Inscription over the place where the bodies of Sts. Peter and Paul were temporarily buried beneath the Basilica of San Sebastiano on the Via Appia, c. 375

✦

Augustine of holy memory . . . never has the slightest breath of suspicion tarnished his name.

—St. Celestine I, c. 430

✦

Let us rejoice, then, dearly beloved, with spiritual joy, and make our boast over the happy end of this illustrious man in the Lord [the martyr St. Lawrence] . . . By his prayer and intercession we trust at all times to be assisted.

—St. Leo I the Great, *Sermon 85*, 450

✦

The death of the martyrs blossoms in the faith of the living.

—St. Gregory I the Great, *Homilies on the Gospels*, c. 590

✦

[St. Mary Magdalen] turned the mass of her crimes into virtues, in order to serve God entirely in penance.

—St. Gregory I the Great, *Homily 33*, c. 590

✦

Like a true lion [leo] he roared, and all the wild beasts trembled; but the sheep gathered close around their shepherd.

—Sergius I, Inscription on the tomb of Pope St. Leo I, 688

✦

These Apostles [St. Peter and St. Paul] came to Rome while yet they were alive, preached here the Word of Life, destroyed error, enlightened souls with the light of truth, and, consummating their martyrdom for the Faith on the same day and together, consecrated the Holy Roman Church by their blood.

—St. Nicholas I, Letter to Emperor Michael III, 863

✦

We honor the servants that honor may redound to the Lord.

—John XV, Canonization of St. Ulrich, 993

✦

Plainly a life such as his, so holy, so passionate, so brilliant, was enough to win [St. Francis of Assisi] a place in the Church Triumphant.

—Gregory IX, *Mira circa nos,* July 16, 1228

✦

God, rewarder of every good . . . granted favors for the exaltation of his ever glorious name to those who asked for them because the clear merits of the virgin Clare [of Assisi] were interceding.

—Innocent IV, Letter to Bartolomeo, Bishop of Spoleto, October 19, 1253

✦

If we look for truth, for learning, and for piety, whom shall we find more learned, wiser, and holier than Augustine?

—Martin V, 1420

✦

Reason, as borne on the wings of Thomas [Aquinas], can scarcely rise higher.

—Leo XIII, *Aeterni Patris,* August 4, 1879

✦

Joseph shines among all mankind by the most august dignity, since by divine will, he was the guardian of the Son of God.

—Leo XIII, *Quamquam Pluries,* August 15, 1889

✦

St. Bernard found no taste in things which did not echo the most sweet Name of Jesus.

—Benedict XV, *Spiritus Paraclitus,* September 15, 1920

✦

The saints have ever been, are, and ever will be the greatest bene-
factors of society, and perfect models for every class and profession,
for every state and condition of life.

—Pius XI, *Divinus Illius Magistri,* December 31, 1929

✦

To [St. Joseph] was entrusted the Divine Child when Herod loosed
his assassins against Him. In a life of faithful performance of everyday duties, he left an example for all those who must gain their
bread by the toil of their hands. He won for himself the title of "The
Just," serving thus as a living model of that Christian justice which
should reign in social life.

—Pius XI, *Divini Redemptoris,* March 19, 1937

✦

We should imitate the virtues of the saints just as they imitated
Christ, for in their virtues there shines forth under different aspects
the splendor of Jesus Christ.

—Pius XII, *Mediator Dei,* November 20, 1947

✦

Martin de Porres was the angel of Lima: the novices went to him
with their doubts, the most serious of the Fathers asked for his
opinions; he brought about reconciliations in marriages, healed the
most stubborn sicknesses, restored peace between enemies, settled
theological disputes and gave his definitive opinion on the most
complicated affairs.

—John XXIII, Address to Pilgrims, May 7, 1962

✦

Remember St. Patrick. Remember what the fidelity of just one man has meant for Ireland and the world.

—John Paul II, Address to the seminarians of St. Patrick's College,
Maynooth, Ireland, October 1, 1979

✦

The saints are those who, having accepted the Paschal Mystery of Christ in faith, now await the final resurrection.

—John Paul II, *Gift and Mystery,* 1996

✦

St. John Mary Vianney astonishes us because in him we can see the power of grace working through human limitations.

—John Paul II, *Gift and Mystery,* 1996

✦

Thérèse [the Little Flower] knew Jesus, loved him and made him loved with the passion of a bride. She penetrated the mysteries of his infancy, the words of his Gospel, the passion of the suffering Servant engraved on his holy Face, in the splendor of his glorious life, in his Eucharistic presence. She sang of all the expressions of Christ's divine charity, as they are presented in the Gospel.

—John Paul II, *Divini Amoris Scientia,* October 19, 1997

✦

The martyrs know that they have found the truth about life in the encounter with Jesus Christ . . . [they] stir in us a profound trust because they give voice to what we already feel and they declare what we would like to have the strength to express.

—John Paul II, *Fides et Ratio,* September 14, 1998

✦

A young woman in search of the truth has become a saint and martyr through the silent workings of divine grace: Teresa Benedicta of the Cross (St. Edith Stein), who from heaven repeats to us today all the words that marked her life: "Far be it from me to glory except in the Cross of our Lord Jesus Christ" (Galatians 6:14).

—John Paul II, Sermon at the Canonization of Edith Stein, October 11, 1998

✦

Blessed Pio of Pietrelcina shared in the Passion with a special intensity: the unique gifts which were given to him, and the interior and mystical sufferings which accompanied them, allowed him constantly to participate in the Lord's agonies, never wavering in his sense that "Calvary is the hill of the saints."

—John Paul II, Sermon at the Beatification of Padre Pio di Pietrelcina,
May 2, 1999

VI

VISIONS OF THE AFTERLIFE

When the prince of pastors shall appear, you shall receive a never-fading crown of glory.

—St. Peter, First Epistle 5:4, c. 45

✦

What shall we say of those things that are being prepared for those who persevere? Only the Creator and Father of the ages, the all-holy One, knows their greatness and beauty.

—St. Clement I, *Letter to the Corinthians,* c. 95

✦

Brethren, we must think of Jesus Christ as God, as judge of quick and dead, and we must not think lightly of our salvation.

—St. Soter, *To the Corinthians,* c. 170

✦

And know, brethren, that the dwelling of our flesh in this world is short and lasts but a little time but the promise of Christ is great and wonderful and so is the rest in the kingdom which is to come and life everlasting.

—St. Soter, *To the Corinthians,* c. 170

✦

God . . . will present the just, as "vessels of mercy prepared before-hand for glory" (Romans 9:23), with the rewards of eternal life; namely, they will live without end in the society of the angels without any fear now of their own fall.

—Pelagius I, Letter to Childebert I, April 557

✦

In the day of judgment no one can excuse himself.

—Pelagius II, Letter to the Schismatic Bishops of Istria, c. 585

✦

Each one will be presented to the Judge exactly as he was when he departed this life. Yet, there must be a cleansing fire before judgment, because of some minor faults that may remain to be purged away.

—St. Gregory I the Great, *Dialogues,* c. 595

✦

A man will not be cleansed in Purgatory of even the least sins, unless during his lifetime he deserved by his good works to receive such favor.

—St. Gregory I the Great, *Dialogues,* 595

✦

There are two kinds of compunction, as you know: one that is afraid of eternal pains, the other that sighs for heavenly rewards.

—St. Gregory I the Great, Letter to Theoctista, 604

✦

The punishment of actual sin is the torture of eternal hell.

—Innocent III, Letter to Humbert, Archbishop of Arles, 1201

✦

I steadfastly hold that there is a purgatory, and that the souls detained there are helped by the acts of intercession of the faithful.

—Pius IV, *Injunctum Nobis,* November 13, 1564

✦

Discover to me, O God, the nothingness of this world, the greatness of heaven, the shortness of time, and the length of eternity.

—Clement XI, *A Universal Prayer,* c. 1715

✦

Only when we have been released from the bonds of this body and "shall see God as He is" (1 John 3:2) shall we understand how closely and wonderfully the divine mercy and justice are linked.

—Pius IX, Allocution to the Sacred College of Cardinals, 1854

✦

The divine design of salvation embraces all men; and those "who without fault on their part do not know the Gospel of Christ and His Church but seek God with a sincere heart, and under the influence of grace endeavor to do His will as recognized through the promptings of their consciences," they too in a number known only to God "can obtain eternal salvation."

—Paul VI, *Credo of the People of God,* June 30, 1968
(quotation from *Lumen Gentium*)

✦

The multitude of those gathered around Jesus and Mary in paradise forms the Church of heaven, where in the enjoyment of eternal beatitude they see God as He is.

—Paul VI, *Credo of the People of God,* June 30, 1968

✦

For the souls in purgatory, waiting for eternal happiness and for meeting the Beloved is a source of suffering, because of the punishment due to sin which separates them from God. But there is also the certitude that once the time of purification is over, the soul will go to meet the One it desires.

—John Paul II, I Urge Catholics to Pray for the Dead, June 2, 1998

VII

THE MASS AND ITS MEANING

Frail, fallen humanity can offer no better act of worship to God than the Mass. It is the most eloquent outpouring of praise and thanksgiving to God, the most potent remedy for all our temporal and spiritual needs, and atones for sin more effectively than any other prayer. The Mass accomplishes all these things because at the altar the priest offers to God the Father the Body and Blood of Jesus Christ. The Mass, then, is the reenactment, the renewal, the representation of the sacrifice Christ made on Calvary. As St. Cyprian (c. 200–258), the martyred bishop of Carthage, wrote, "The Passion of the Lord is the Sacrifice we offer."

As long as humankind has had an inkling that there is a Supreme Being, people have offered sacrifices. When Jesus was physically present on earth, pious Jews brought live sheep, goats, bulls, even doves, to the Temple in Jerusalem. There the servants of the priests took the creatures and killed them, then the priests offered the slain victims to God. That is what sacrifice meant in Judaism two thousand years ago: a living creature slain and offered to God.

Christ's death on the Cross was the perfect sacrifice. It had the perfect victim, Christ himself, who went to his death at the hands of evil men as meekly as any lamb slain in the Temple. It had the perfect priest—again, Christ himself—who offered himself to the Father for our sake.

Christ's death on the Cross accomplished three things once and for all: it atoned for the sins of the entire human race; it healed the breach that had existed between God and humankind since the Fall; and it opened wide the gates of heaven.

The Mass is the ongoing memorial of our redemption, of Christ's sacrifice on the Cross. And what we do on earth, Christ does in heaven. Day after day he stands before the Father, his Body still bearing the marks of his Passion, an eternal reminder of what he suffered to appease the just wrath of God and gain forgiveness and salvation for humankind. St. John describes the scene for us: "Behold in the midst of the throne and of the four living creatures, and in the midst of the ancients, a Lamb standing as it were slain" (Apocalypse 5:6).

When a priest offers the Mass, he is showing the Father, reminding the Father as it were, of what the Son wrought for us. Archbishop Fulton J. Sheen put it this way: "The Mass is . . . the only Holy Act which keeps the wrath of God from a sinful world, because it holds the Cross between heaven and earth, thus renewing that decisive moment when our sad and tragic humanity journeyed suddenly forth to the fullness of supernatural life."

Furthermore, the Mass is a sign of the unity of the Church. It is the dramatic expression that "we, being many, are one bread, one body" (1 Corinthians 10:17).

At the heart of the Mass is a miracle. Over the bread and wine the priest repeats the same words that Christ spoke at the Last Supper: "This is my body . . . this is my blood." At these words of consecration, ordinary bread and wine become truly the Body and Blood, soul and divinity, of Jesus Christ, the Second Person of the Blessed Trinity. It is an inestimable gift to humankind, and an inexpressible mystery.

We look at the bread and the wine before and after the priest has spoken the words of consecration over them and they look, taste, smell, and feel like bread and wine. But they are not. Their substance has changed into Christ's very own Body and Blood (hence the term "transubstantiation"). Christ is truly present on the altar (hence the phrase, "Real Presence"). Our senses cannot grasp the miracle that has taken place, but faith can.

"Do this for a commemoration of me" (Luke 2:19), Christ said at the Last Supper, and the Church has fulfilled that command faithfully ever since. Both the Acts of the Apostles and the letters of St. Paul tell us that when the first Christians gathered together to pray, they repeated the words and actions of Christ at the Last Supper. Furthermore, we know that the doctrine of the Real Presence was already firmly understood in the earliest days of the Church: St. Paul himself writes, "Is not the cup of blessing we bless a sharing in the blood of Christ? And is not the bread we break a sharing in the body of Christ?" (1 Corinthians 10:16).

Father Joseph A. Jungmann, the twentieth century's greatest historian of the Mass, writes, "Christ Himself gave us only the essential core of the liturgical celebration; the externals had to be furnished by men. These the Church has worked out by slow development, year by year." By the end of the sixth century, the essential outline of the Mass and most of its prayers were in place. Through all the centuries that followed, the popes were the careful guardians of the Mass. Even those popes who debased themselves and their sacred office did not dare to touch the Mass.

Then something unprecedented occurred in 1969. Pope Paul VI promulgated the *Novus Ordo Missae*, the New Order of the Mass. For the first time in the history of the Catholic Church, a manufactured liturgy was imposed upon the faithful.

The scale of the changes to the Mass was staggering. The *Novus Ordo* was not a simple translation of the Latin prayers into the

"A striking departure from the Catholic theology of the Holy Mass"

Almost three months before Pope Paul VI made the Novus Ordo Missae binding on all Catholics, two cardinals, Alfredo Ottaviani and Antonio Bacci, sent the following letter expressing their grave reservations regarding the theology of the new Mass and the impact it would have on the faithful. Pope Paul disregarded their warning.

✦

Most Holy Father,

Having examined, and presented for the scrutiny of others, the *Novus Ordo Missae* prepared by the experts of the *Consilium ad exsequendam Constitutionem de Sacra Liturgia*, and after lengthy reflection and prayer, we feel it to be our duty in the sight of God and towards Your Holiness to put forward the following considerations:

1. The accompanying critical study is the work of a group of theologians, liturgists, and pastors of souls. Brief though it is, it sufficiently demonstrates that the *Novus Ordo Missae*—considering the new elements, susceptible of widely differing evaluations, which appear to be implied or taken for granted—represents, as a whole and in detail, a striking departure from the Catholic theology of the Holy Mass as it was formulated in Session XXII of the Council of Trent, which, by fixing definitively the canons of the rite, erected an insurmountable barrier against any heresy which might attack the integrity of the Mystery.

2. The pastoral reasons adduced in support of such a grave break—even if they could stand up in the face of doctrinal reasons—do not appear sufficient. The innovations in the *Novus Ordo Missae*, and on the other hand the things of eternal value relegated to an inferior or different place (if indeed they are still to be found at all), could well turn into a certainty the suspicion, already prevalent, alas, in many circles, that truths which have always been believed by Christians can be altered or silenced without infidelity to that sacred deposit of doctrine to which the Catholic faith is bound forever. Recent reforms have amply shown that fresh changes in the liturgy could not but lead to utter bewilderment on the part of the faithful, who are already giving signs of restiveness and of an indubitable lessening of faith. Amongst the best of the clergy, the practical result is an agonizing crisis of conscience of which numberless instances come to our notice daily.

3. We are certain that these considerations, which spring from the living voice of shepherds and flock, cannot but find an echo in the paternal heart of Your Holiness, always so profoundly solicitous for the spiritual needs of the children of the Church. The subjects for whose benefit a law is passed have always had—more than the right—the duty, if it should instead prove harmful, of asking the legislator with filial trust for its abrogation.

Therefore we most earnestly beseech Your Holiness not to deprive us—at a time of such painful divisions and ever-increasing perils for the purity of the Faith and the unity of the Church, daily and sorrowfully echoed in the voice of our common Father—of the possibility of continuing to have recourse to the fruitful integrity of that *Missale Romanum* of St. Pius V, so highly praised by Your Holiness and so deeply venerated and loved by the whole Catholic world.

Alfredo Cardinal Ottaviani and Antonio Cardinal Bacci
Feast of St. Pius X (September 3, 1969)

vernacular. This was a wholesale rewrite of the text of the Mass and a complete revision of the rubrics of the ritual. The timeless poetry and splendor of the Mass was tossed aside and a mundane, prosaic liturgy was put in its place. Even the ceremonies of Holy Week, the most solemn and moving of the Church year, were rendered insipid. Many of the Catholic faithful, to say nothing of the priests and religious, were bewildered, even stunned, by the *Novus Ordo*. And the changes never stopped.

From the day the *Novus Ordo* was put in place, many priests have taken the liberty of altering the text and the ritual according to whim. Parish "Liturgy Committees" continue to invent a host of innovations that range from the banal to the bizarre to the blasphemous. In the overwhelming majority of Catholic parishes, solemnity, mystery, even beauty, have disappeared. Those parishes that do celebrate the Mass reverently are so rare as to invite comment.

And if the Mass could be tampered with, certainly the churches and chapels in which the Mass was celebrated would not be spared. In the decades since the *Novus Ordo* was introduced, the Catholic faithful have seen their sanctuaries gutted, high altars and communion rails ripped out, statues, pictures, and shrines removed or tucked into out-of-the-way places. Not since the Reformation has Catholicism suffered such an outburst of iconoclasm.

Worse still has been the fate of the tabernacle in which the Blessed Sacrament is reserved: in many churches it is relegated to a back room or pushed into an obscure corner as if it were an embarrassing relic.

Catholics who have gone to their pastors and bishops to protest these excesses are generally regarded with pity, contempt, or even open hostility.

Most heartbreaking is the impact these changes have had on the religious formation of those Catholics who still go to church. A poll reported in *The New York Times* found that seventy percent of all Catholics in America do not believe in the Real Presence. After thirty years of seeing the Eucharist treated in a casual, offhand, even irreverent manner, how could they conclude anything else?

One cannot believe that this is what Paul VI had in mind when he commanded that all churches of the Latin rite celebrate the *Novus Ordo Missae*. Nonetheless, wittingly or unwittingly, he unleashed the whirlwind.

It is a relief to report that since 1969 there have been Catholic priests, religious, and laity who labored to keep the traditional Latin rite alive. In those early years, Paul VI would not sanction the continuance of the traditional rite (he granted exceptions only to elderly or ailing priests, and, strange to say, to the Catholics of England and Wales). In spite of this, the traditional Latin Mass survived as an underground movement. Then, in 1988, Pope John Paul II issued a document known as *Ecclesia Dei*, which recognized "the rightful aspirations" of those "Catholic faithful who feel attached to some previous liturgical and disciplinary forms of the Latin tradition." Since then, the traditional Latin Mass movement has expanded at a tremendous rate. In the wake of *Ecclesia Dei,* new traditionalist religious orders of priests and nuns have been founded with Vatican approval, and they are flourishing.

In spite of the successes of the traditionalists, at this moment the *Novus Ordo* liturgy and its promoters seem unstoppable. It appears that nothing can make them rethink their position: not the religious malformation of the faithful, nor the drop in Mass attendance, nor the precipitous decline in religious vocations, nor the number of religious orders that are on the verge of extinction, nor the en masse closing of Catholic schools. How long this will continue, only God knows.

Under these circumstances, the best that traditionalist Catholics can hope for is recognition from Rome that they are a distinct rite within the Catholic Church. The Church has always embraced a variety of liturgical traditions; the Ukrainians, the Melkites, the Maronites, the Greek Catholics—to name just a few—preserve their ancient liturgies while remaining in union with Rome. A Latin rite would eliminate the tension that too often exists between traditionalist Catholics and their local bishops. Most important, it would safeguard the Mass of the ages.

✦ ✦ ✦

The Lord . . . has commanded the offerings and services to be carried out not carelessly or disorderly, but at fixed times and seasons. He has himself fixed according to his surpassing counsel where and by whom he desires them to be performed, in order that all things may be done in holy fashion according to his good pleasure and acceptable to his will.

—St. Clement I, *Letter to the Corinthians,* c. 95

✦

For when the Lord says, "Unless ye have eaten the flesh of the Son of Man, and drunk His blood, ye will not have life in you; you ought so to be partakers at the Holy Table, as to have no doubt whatever concerning the reality of Christ's Body and Blood.

—St. Leo I the Great, *Sermon 91*, c. 461

✦

It is His Body that is there taken, His Flesh that is divided for the salvation of the people, His Blood that is poured, not as before into the hands of unbelievers, but into the mouths of the faithful.

—St. Gregory I the Great, *Dialogues,* c. 600

✦

For what Christian can doubt that at the very hour of the offering, at the words of the priest, the heavens are opened, the choirs of angels are present in that mystery of Jesus Christ, the lowest things are knit with the highest, the earthly things are united with the heavenly, the visible and the invisible are made one?

—St. Gregory I the Great, *Dialogues,* c. 600

✦

Not only do the priests offer the sacrifice, but also all the faithful: for what the priest does personally by virtue of his ministry, the faithful do collectively by virtue of their intention.

—Innocent III, *De Sacro Altaris Mysterio*, c. 1200

✦

After the words of consecration there is present numerically the same Body of Christ as was born of the Virgin and was immolated on the Cross.

—Clement VI, Letter to the Armenians, September 29, 1351

✦

Hail true Body, born of the Virgin Mary; suffering, sacrificed truly on the Cross for mankind; from whose pierced side flowed water and blood. Be merciful to us at the judgment of death, O sweet Jesus, O merciful Jesus, O Jesus Son of Mary.

—Attributed to Innocent VI, *Ave Verum Corpus,* c. 1357

✦

In the Mass there is offered to God a true sacrifice, properly speaking, which is propitiatory for the living and the dead.

—Pius IV, *Injunctum Nobis,* November 13, 1564

✦

By virtue of Our Apostolic authority We give and grant in perpetuity that for the singing or reading of Mass in any church whatsoever, this Missal may be followed absolutely, without any scruple of conscience or fear of incurring any penalty, judgment or censure, and may be freely and lawfully used.

—St. Pius V, *Quo Primum*, July 14, 1570

✦

Nor shall bishops, administrators, canons, chaplains, and other secular priests, or religious of whatsoever Order or by whatsoever title designated, be obliged to celebrate Mass otherwise than enjoined by Us. We likewise order and declare that no one whosoever shall be forced or coerced into altering this Missal and that this present Constitution can never be revoked or modified, but shall forever remain valid and have the force of law.

—St. Pius V, *Quo Primum*, July 14, 1570

✦

There is indeed nothing which is more contrary to, or bad for, church discipline, than negligently and disrespectfully to carry out liturgical worship.

—Benedict XIV, *Annus Qui Hunc*, February 19, 1749

✦

Christ's love towards men was so great that not only was He willing to endure most cruel sufferings for our salvation and an atrocious death on the cross, but also He wished to nourish us eternally in the sacrament of His body and blood.

—Pius IX, *Amantissimi Redemptoris*, May 3, 1858

✦

[Christ] decreed that that same sacrifice which He performed . . . be renewed and take place daily by the ministry of the priesthood . . . that the salvific and most abundant fruits of His passion might forever be dispersed upon mankind.

—Pius IX, *Amantissimi Redemptoris*, May 3, 1858

✦

By this oblation God is pleased and, granting the grace and gift of repentance, remits even great crimes and sins. Although grievously offended by our sins, He is moved from anger to mercy, from the severity of just chastisement to clemency; by it the title and obligation of temporal punishment is dissolved; by it the souls of the departed in Christ who have not yet been fully purged are aided; by it temporal goods also are obtained, if they do not stand in the way of greater benefits; by it singular honor and cult are procured for the saints and especially for the Immaculate and most holy Mother of God, the Virgin Mary.

—Pius IX, *Amantissimi Redemptoris*, May 3, 1858

✦

[The Mass] should be celebrated with the proper splendor of sacred ceremonies and rites so that the greatness of this mystery will shine forth all the more even from external appearances.

—Pius IX, *Amantissimi Redemptoris,* May 3, 1858

✦

Faith likewise teaches us to acknowledge Him and to worship Him as really present in the Eucharist, as verily abiding through all time in the midst of men.

—Leo XIII, *Mirae Caritatis,* May 28, 1902

✦

Very beautiful and joyful too is the spectacle of Christian brotherhood and social equality which is afforded when men of all conditions, gentle and simple, rich and poor, learned and unlearned, gather round the holy altar, all sharing alike in this heavenly banquet.

—Leo XIII, *Mirae Caritatis,* May 28, 1902

✦

Genuine charity . . . leaps forth with all the heat and energy of a flame from the Most Holy Eucharist in which Christ Himself is present and lives.

—Leo XIII, *Mirae Caritatis,* May 28, 1902

✦

Infinite in value and infinitely accessible is the gift which we present to the Father in His only begotten Son.

—Leo XIII, *Mirae Caritatis,* May 28, 1902

✦

He who approaches the Holy Table should do so, not out of routine, or vain-glory, or human respect, but that he wishes to please God, to be more closely united with Him by charity, and to have recourse to this divine remedy for his weaknesses and defects.

—St. Pius X, *Sacra Tridentina Synodus,* December 20, 1905

✦

It is plain that by the frequent or daily reception of the Holy Eucharist, union with Christ is strengthened, the spiritual life more abundantly sustained, the soul more richly endowed with virtues, and the pledge of everlasting happiness more securely bestowed on the recipient.

—St. Pius X, *Sacra Tridentina Synodus,* December 20, 1905

✦

Christ is present at the august sacrifice of the altar both in the person of His minister and above all under the Eucharistic species.

—Pius XII, *Mediator Dei,* November 20, 1947

✦

The Church has further used her right of control over liturgical observance to protect the purity of divine worship against abuse from dangerous and imprudent innovations introduced by private individuals and particular churches.

—Pius XII, *Mediator Dei,* November 20, 1947

✦

Private individuals, therefore, even though they be clerics, may not be left to decide for themselves in these holy and venerable matters.

—Pius XII, Mediator Dei, November 20, 1947

✦

The temerity and daring of those who introduce novel liturgical practices, or call for the revival of obsolete rites out of harmony with prevailing laws and rubrics, deserve severe reproof.

—Pius XII, Mediator Dei, November 20, 1947

✦

One would be straying from the straight path were he to wish the altar restored to its primitive table form; were he to want black excluded as a color for the liturgical vestments; were he to forbid the use of sacred images and statues in Churches; were he to order the crucifix so designed that the divine Redeemer's body shows no trace of His cruel sufferings; and lastly were he to disdain and reject polyphonic music or singing in parts.

—Pius XII, Mediator Dei, November 20, 1947

✦

The august sacrifice of the altar, then, is no mere empty commemoration of the passion and death of Jesus Christ, but a true and proper act of sacrifice, whereby the High Priest by an unbloody immolation offers Himself a most acceptable victim to the Eternal Father, as He did upon the cross.

—Pius XII, Mediator Dei, November 20, 1947

✦

Priests and beloved sons, we hold in our hands a great treasure, a precious pearl, the inexhaustible riches of the blood of Jesus Christ.

—Pius XII, *Menti Nostrae,* September 23, 1950

✦

The Catholic Church has a dignity far surpassing that of every merely human society, for it was founded by Christ the Lord. It is altogether fitting, therefore, that the language it uses should be noble, majestic, and *non-vernacular* (emphasis from the original).

—John XXIII, *Veterum Sapientia,* February 22, 1962

✦

[Latin] is also a most effective bond, binding the Church of today with that of the past and of the future in wonderful continuity.

—John XXIII, *Veterum Sapientia,* February 22, 1962

✦

The employment of Latin has recently been contested in many quarters, and many are asking what the mind of the Apostolic See is in this matter. We have therefore decided . . . to ensure that the ancient and uninterrupted use of Latin be maintained and, where necessary, restored.

—John XXIII, *Veterum Sapientia,* February 22, 1962

✦

In the exercise of their paternal care [bishops and superiors-general of religious orders] shall be on their guard lest anyone under their jurisdiction, eager for revolutionary changes, writes against the use of Latin in the teaching of the higher sacred studies or in the liturgy, or through prejudice makes light of the Holy See's will in this regard or interprets it falsely.

—John XXIII, *Veterum Sapientia*, February 22, 1962

✦

The reform which is about to be brought into being . . . is not an arbitrary act. It is not a transitory or optional experiment. It is not some dilettante's improvisation. It is a law. It has been thought out by authoritative experts of sacred Liturgy; it has been discussed and meditated upon for a long time. We shall do well to accept it with joyful interest and put it into practice punctually, unanimously and carefully.

—Paul VI, Address to a General Audience, November 19, 1969

✦

The unity of the Lord's Supper, of the Sacrifice on the cross of the re-presentation and the renewal of both in the Mass, is inviolably affirmed and celebrated in the new rite just as they were in the old. The Mass is and remains the memorial of Christ's Last Supper. At that Supper the Lord changed the bread and wine into His Body and His Blood, and instituted the Sacrifice of the New Testament.

—Paul VI, Address to a General Audience, November 19, 1969

✦

[Christ] willed that the Sacrifice should be identically renewed by the power of His Priesthood, conferred on the Apostles. Only the manner of offering is different, namely, an unbloody and sacramental manner; and it is offered in perennial memory of Himself, until His final return.

— Paul VI, Address to a General Audience, November 19, 1969

✦

"This many-sided inconvenience"

On November 26, 1969, four days before the new Mass would be introduced, Pope Paul VI explained to a General Audience why he had decided to alter the immemorial Latin rite.

✦

Our Dear Sons and Daughters:

1. We ask you to turn your minds once more to the liturgical innovation of the new rite of the Mass. This new rite will be introduced into our celebration of the holy Sacrifice starting from Sunday next which is the first of Advent, November 30 (in Italy).

2. A new rite of the Mass: a change in a venerable tradition that has gone on for centuries. This is something that affects our hereditary religious patrimony, which seemed to enjoy the privilege of being untouchable and settled. It seemed to bring the prayer of our forefathers and our saints to our lips and to give us the comfort of feeling faithful to our spiritual past, which we kept alive to pass it on to the generations ahead.

3. It is at such a moment as this that we get a better understanding of the value of historical tradition and the communion of the saints. This change will affect the ceremonies of the Mass. We shall become aware, perhaps with some feeling of annoyance, that the ceremonies at the altar are no longer being carried out with the same words and gestures to which

continued

we were accustomed—perhaps so much accustomed that we no longer took any notice of them. This change also touches the faithful. It is intended to interest each one of those present, to draw them out of their customary personal devotions or their usual torpor.

4. We must prepare for this many-sided inconvenience. It is the kind of upset caused by every novelty that breaks in on our habits. We shall notice that pious persons are disturbed most, because they have their own respectable way of hearing Mass, and they will feel shaken out of their usual thoughts and obliged to follow those of others. Even priests may feel some annoyance in this respect.

5. So what is to be done on this special and historical occasion? First of all, we must prepare ourselves. This novelty is no small thing. We should not let ourselves be surprised by the nature, or even the nuisance, of its exterior forms. As intelligent persons and conscientious faithful, we should find out as much as we can about this innovation. It will not be hard to do so, because of the many fine efforts being made by the Church and by publishers. As we said on another occasion, we shall do well to take into account the motives for this grave change. The first is obedience to the Council. That obedience now implies obedience to the Bishops, who interpret the Council's prescription and put them into practice.

6. This first reason is not simply canonical—relating to an external precept. It is connected with the charism of the liturgical act. In other words, it is linked with the power and efficacy of the Church's prayer, the most authoritative utter-

ance of which comes from the Bishop. This is also true of priests, who help the Bishop in his ministry, and like him act *in persona Christi.* It is Christ's will, it is the breath of the Holy Spirit which calls the Church to make this change. A prophetic moment is occurring in the mystical body of Christ, which is the Church. This moment is shaking the Church, arousing it, obliging it to renew the mysterious art of its prayer.

7. The other reason for the reform is this renewal of prayer. It is aimed at associating the assembly of the faithful more closely and more effectively with the official rite, that of the Word and that of the Eucharistic Sacrifice, that constitutes the Mass. For the faithful are also invested with the "royal priesthood"; that is, they are qualified to have supernatural conversation with God.

8. It is here that the greatest newness is going to be noticed, the newness of language. No longer Latin, but the spoken language will be the principal language of the Mass. The introduction of the vernacular will certainly be a great sacrifice for those who know the beauty, the power and the expressive sacrality of Latin. We are parting with the speech of the Christian centuries; we are becoming like profane intruders in the literary preserve of sacred utterance. We will lose a great part of that stupendous and incomparable artistic and spiritual thing, the Gregorian chant.

9. We have reason indeed for regret, reason almost for bewilderment. What can we put in the place of that language

continued

of the angels? We are giving up something of priceless worth. But why? What is more precious than these loftiest of our Church's values?

10. The answer will seem banal, prosaic. Yet it is a good answer, because it is human, because it is apostolic.

11. Understanding of prayer is worth more than the silken garments in which it is royally dressed. Participation by the people is worth more—particularly participation by modern people, so fond of plain language which is easily understood and converted into everyday speech.

12. If the divine Latin language kept us apart from the children, from youth, from the world of labor and of affairs, if it were a dark screen, not a clear window, would it be right for us fishers of souls to maintain it as the exclusive language of prayer and religious intercourse? What did St. Paul have to say about that? Read chapter 14 of the first letter to the Corinthians: "In Church I would rather speak five words with my mind, in order to instruct others, than ten thousand words in a tongue" (1 Corinthians 14:19).

13. St. Augustine seems to be commenting on this when he says, "Have no fear of teachers, so long as all are instructed." But, in any case, the new rite of the Mass provides that the faithful "should be able to sing together, in Latin, at least the parts of the Ordinary of the Mass, especially the Creed and the Lord's Prayer, the Our Father" (*Sacrosanctum Concilium* *n. 19*).

14. But, let us bear this well in mind, for our counsel and our comfort: the Latin language will not thereby disappear. It will continue to be the noble language of the Holy See's official acts; it will remain as the means of teaching in ecclesiastical studies and as the key to the patrimony of our religious, historical and human culture. If possible, it will reflourish in splendor.

15. Finally, if we look at the matter properly, we shall see that the fundamental outline of the Mass is still the traditional one, not only theologically but also spiritually. Indeed, if the rite is carried out as it ought to be, the spiritual aspect will be found to have greater richness. The greater simplicity of the ceremonies, the variety and abundance of scriptural texts, the joint acts of the ministers, the silences which will mark various deeper moments in the rite, will all help to bring this out.

16. But two indispensable requirements above all will make that richness clear: a profound participation by every single one present, and an outpouring of spirit in community charity. These requirements will help to make the Mass more than ever a school of spiritual depth and a peaceful but demanding school of Christian sociology. The soul's relationship with Christ and with the brethren thus attains new and vital intensity. Christ, the victim and the priest, renews and offers up his redeeming sacrifice through the ministry of the Church in the symbolic rite of his last supper. He leaves us his body and blood under the appear

continued

ances of bread and wine, for our personal and spiritual nourishment, for our fusion in the unity of his redeeming love and his immortal life.

17. But there is still a practical difficulty, which the excellence of the sacred renders not a little important. How can we celebrate this new rite when we have not yet got a complete missal, and there are still so many uncertainties about what to do?

18. To conclude, it will be helpful to read to you some directions from the competent office, namely the Sacred Congregation for Divine Worship. Here they are:

"As regards the obligation of the rite:"

1. For the Latin text: Priests who celebrate in Latin, in private or also in public, in cases provided for by the legislation, may use either the Roman Missal or the new rite until November 28, 1971. If they use the Roman Missal, they may nevertheless make use of the three new anaphoras and the Roman Canon, having regard to the provisions respecting the last text (omission of some saints, conclusions, etc.). They may moreover recite the readings and the prayer of the faithful in the vernacular. If they use the new rite, they must follow the official text, with the concessions as regards the vernacular indicated above.

2. For the vernacular text. In Italy, all those who celebrate in the presence of the people from November 30

next, must use the *Rito della Messa* published by the Italian Episcopal Conference or by another National Conference. On feast days, readings shall be taken: either from the Lectionary published by the Italian Center for Liturgical Action, or from the Roman Missal for feast days, as in use heretofore. On ferial days, the ferial Lectionary published three years ago shall continue to be used. No problem arises for those who celebrate in private, because they must celebrate in Latin. If a priest celebrates in the vernacular by special indult, as regards the texts, he shall follow what was said above for the Mass with the people; but for the rite he shall follow the *Ordo* published by the Italian Episcopal Conference.

19. In every case, and at all times, let us remember that "the Mass is a Mystery to be lived in a death of Love. Its divine reality surpasses all words. . . . It is the Action par excellence, the very act of our Redemption, in the Memorial which makes it present" (Zundel).

With Our Apostolic Benediction.

It is necessary that all the pastors and other faithful have a new awareness, not only of the lawfulness but also of the richness for the church of a diversity of charisms, traditions of spirituality and apostolate, which also constitutes the beauty of unity in variety.

—John Paul II, *Ecclesia Dei*, July 2, 1988

✦

To all those Catholic faithful who feel attached to some previous liturgical and disciplinary forms of the Latin tradition, I wish to manifest my will to facilitate their ecclesial communion by means of the necessary measures to guarantee respect for their rightful aspirations. In this matter I ask for the support of the bishops and of all those engaged in the pastoral ministry in the church.

—John Paul II, *Ecclesia Dei*, July 2, 1988

✦

Respect must everywhere be shown for the feelings of all those who are attached to the Latin liturgical tradition by a wide and generous application of the directives already issued some time ago by the Apostolic See for the use of the Roman Missal according to the typical edition of 1962.

—John Paul II, *Ecclesia Dei*, July 2, 1988

VIII

THE SEVEN SACRAMENTS

Baptism

Be baptized every one of you in the name of Jesus Christ for the remission of your sins: and you shall receive the gift of the Holy Ghost.

—St. Peter, Acts of the Apostles 2:38, c. 30

✦

Whoever has been baptized anywhere in the name of Christ, at once obtains the grace of Christ.

—St. Stephen I, c. 255

✦

We also desire that babes who for their youth are not yet able to speak and persons in any extremity who need the sacred wave of baptism should be succored with all speed, lest we risk the destruction of our own souls by denying the font of salvation to those who seek it.

—St. Siricius, Letter to Bishop Himerius of Tarragona, 385

✦

If anyone threatened with shipwreck, or the attack of enemies, or the uncertainties of a siege, or anyone put in a hopeless condition due to some bodily sickness, also for what in his faith is his only help [baptism], let him receive at the very moment of his request the reward of the regeneration he begs for. Enough of past mistakes!

—St. Siricius, Letter to Bishop Himerius of Tarragona, 385

{*Pope Siricius was addressing the inflexibility of some priests who would only baptize during the Easter season, no matter what the emergency.*}

✦

And because of the transgression of the first man, the whole stock of the human race was tainted; no one can be set free from the state of the old Adam save through Christ's sacrament of baptism.

—St. Leo I the Great, *Letter 15*, July 21, 447

✦

The water of baptism is like the Virgin's womb; for the same Holy Spirit fills the font, Who filled the Virgin, that the sin, which that sacred conception overthrew, may be taken away by this mystical washing."

—St. Leo I the Great, *Sermon 24*, 461

✦

Whoever says, then, that sins are not entirely put away in baptism, let him say that the Egyptians did not really die in the Red Sea.

—St. Gregory I the Great, Letter to St. Leander of Seville, c. 595

✦

Through the sacrament of baptism the guilt [of original sin] is remitted and one also reaches the Kingdom of Heaven, whose gate the blood of Christ mercifully opened to His faithful.

—Innocent III, Letter to Humbert, Archbishop of Arles, 1201

✦

Holy baptism, which is the gateway to the spiritual life, holds the first place among all the sacraments.

—Eugenius IV, *Exultate Deo,* November 22, 1439

Confession

It is better for a man to confess his sins than to harden his heart.

— St. Clement I, *Letter to the Corinthians,* c. 95

✦

Since God is the knower of the heart, at no time must penance be denied to him who asks for it.

—St. Celestine I, Letter to the Bishops of Vienne and Narbonne, 428

✦

Jesus Christ gave to those who held authority in the Church the power to grant the discipline of penance to those who confess and, after they have been purified through salutary satisfaction, to admit them to the communion of the sacraments through the door of reconciliation.

—St. Leo I the Great, Letter to Theodore, Bishop of Forum Julii, June 11, 452

✦

With regard to penance, what is demanded of the faithful is clearly not that an acknowledgment of the nature of individual sins written in a little book be read publicly, since it suffices that the states of conscience be made known to the priests alone in secret confession.

—St. Leo I the Great, *Letter 168,* March 6, 459

✦

A greater number will be induced to penance only if the conscience of the penitent is not made public for all to hear.

—St. Leo I the Great, *Letter 168,* March 6, 459

✦

To do penance is to bewail the evil we have done.

—St. Gregory I the Great, *Homilies on the Gospels,* c. 590

✦

A Christian is bound by a necessity of salvation to confess only to [a priest], and not to one or more laymen, however good and devout they may be.

—Martin V, *Inter Cunctus,* 1418

✦

The Sacrament of Penance [is] the masterpiece of God's goodness.

—Pius XII, *Menti Nostrae,* September 23, 1950

✦

The Christ who calls us to the Eucharistic banquet is always the same Christ who exhorts us to penance.

—John Paul II, *Redemptor Hominis*, March 4, 1979

Holy Communion

When the Lord says, "Unless ye have eaten the flesh of the Son of Man, and drunk His blood, ye will not have life in you," you ought so to be partakers at the Holy Table, as to have no doubt whatever concerning the reality of Christ's Body and Blood.

—St. Leo I the Great, *Sermon 91,* 461

✦

Among the weapons against the prince of this world . . . the most potent is . . . a frequent partaking of the Lord's Body.

—St. Gregory VII, Letter to Matilda of Tuscany, February 16, 1074

✦

The effect of this sacrament [the Eucharist] which He operates in the soul of him who takes it worthily is the union of man with Christ.

—Eugenius IV, *Exultate Deo,* November 22, 1439

✦

In the most Holy Sacrament of the Eucharist the body and blood together with the soul and divinity of our Lord Jesus Christ are truly, really, and substantially present.

—Pius IV, *Injunctum Nobis*, November 13, 1564

✦

There is a difference between the food of the body and that of the soul, that whereas the former is changed into our substance, the latter changes us into its own.

—Leo XIII, *Mira Caritatis,* May 28, 1902

✦

By this Sacrament faith is fed, in it the mind finds its nourishment, the objections of the rationalists are brought to naught, and abundant light is thrown on the supernatural order.

—Leo XIII, *Mira Caritatis,* May 28, 1902

✦

The faithful, being united to God by means of the Sacrament, may thence derive strength to resist their sensual passions, to cleanse themselves from the stains of daily faults, and to avoid those grave sins to which human frailty is liable.

—St. Pius X, Sacra Tridentina Synodus, December 20, 1905

✦

In the profound vision which he had of the Church as a society, Pope Pius X recognized that it was the Blessed Sacrament which had the power to nourish her intimate life substantially, and to elevate her high above all other human societies.

—Pius XII, Quest' ore di fulgente, May 29, 1954

Confirmation

The . . . Holy Spirit comes to you today in the Sacrament of Confirmation, to involve you more completely in the Church's fight against sin and in her mission of fostering holiness. He comes to dwell more fully in your hearts and to strengthen you for the struggle with evil.

—John Paul II, The Seven Sacraments, October 1982

✦

The seal of the Holy Spirit therefore signifies and brings about the disciple's total belonging to Jesus Christ, his being always at the latter's service in the Church, and at the same time it implies the promise of divine protection in the trials he will have to endure to witness to his faith in the world.

—John Paul II, Confirmation Seals Us With Gift of the Spirit,
October 21, 1998

Matrimony

The Truth [Christ] absolutely forbids a man to put away his wife, save only for adultery.

> —St. Gregory VII, Letter to the Bishop and People of Genoa,
> February 26, 1074

✦

It is clear that marriage, even in the state of nature and certainly long before it was raised to the dignity of a sacrament, was divinely instituted in such a way that it should be a perpetual and indissoluble bond, which cannot therefore be dissolved by any civil bond.

> —Pius VI, Letter to the Bishop of Agria, July 11, 1789

✦

Marriage has God for its Author.

> —Leo XIII, *Arcanum Divinae Sapientiae*, February 10, 1880

✦

No law of man can abolish the natural and primeval right of marriage, or in any way set aside the chief purpose of matrimony established in the beginning by the authority of God: "Increase and multiply."

> —Leo XIII, *Rerum Novarum*, May 15, 1891

✦

Each individual marriage, inasmuch as it is a conjugal union of a particular man and woman, arises only from the free consent of each of the spouses; and this free act of the will, by which each party hands over and accepts those rights proper to the state of marriage, is so necessary to constitute true marriage that it cannot be supplied by any human power.

—Pius XI, *Casti Connubii,* December 31, 1930

✦

Marriage is not, then, the effect of chance or the product of evolution of unconscious natural forces; it is the wise institution of the Creator to realize in mankind His design of love.

—Paul VI, *Humanae Vitae,* July 25, 1968

✦

The sacredness of Christian marriage consists in the fact that in God's plan the marriage covenant between a man and a woman becomes the image and symbol of the covenant which unites God and his people.

—John Paul II, Address at Williams-Brice Stadium, South Carolina, September 11, 1987

✦

A man and woman joined in matrimony become partners in a divine undertaking: through the act of procreation, God's gift is accepted and a new life opens to the future.

—John Paul II, *Evangelium Vitae,* March 25, 1995

Holy Orders

With respect to the priests of the Lord whom we have heard you aid against the plots of wicked men, and whose cause you sustain, know ye that in so doing ye please God greatly, who has called them to the service of Himself, and has honored them with so intimate a fellowship with Him, that through them He accepts the oblations of others, and pardons their sins, and reconciles them with Him.

—St. Pontian, Letter to Felix Subscribonius, c. 233

✦

All we priests and Levites are bound by the unbreakable law of [Christ's] instructions to subdue our hearts and bodies to soberness and modesty from the day of our ordination, that we may be wholly pleasing to our God in the sacrifices which we daily offer.

—St. Siricius, Letter to Bishop Himerius of Tarragona, 385

✦

Anyone who believes and contends that he can perform the Sacrifice of the Eucharist without having first been ordained by a bishop as mentioned above is a heretic.

—Innocent III, *Profession of Faith Prescribed for the Waldensians*, 1208

✦

The priesthood of Jesus Christ is a living and continuous reality through all the ages to the end of time.

—Pius XII, *Mediator Dei*, November 20, 1947

✦

Only to the apostles, and thenceforth to those on whom their successors have imposed hands, is granted the power of the priesthood. . . . This priesthood is not transmitted by heredity or human descent. It does not emanate from the Christian community. It is not a delegation from the people. . . . It is entirely supernatural. It comes from God.

—Pius XII, *Mediator Dei*, November 20, 1947

✦

The priest is like "another Christ" because he is marked with an indelible character making him, as it were, a living image of our Savior.

—Pius XII, *Menti Nostrae,* September 23, 1950

✦

[The Catholic Church] holds that it is not admissible to ordain women to the priesthood, for very fundamental reasons. These reasons include: the example recorded in the Sacred Scriptures of Christ choosing his Apostles only from among men; the constant practice of the Church, which has imitated Christ in choosing only men; and her living teaching authority which has consistently held that the exclusion of women from the priesthood is in accordance with God's plan for his Church.

—Paul VI, Response to the Letter of His Grace the Most Reverend Dr. F. D. Coggan, Archbishop of Canterbury, concerning the Ordination of Women to the Priesthood, November 30, 1975

✦

The Church has no authority whatsoever to confer priestly ordination on women and . . . this judgment is to be definitively held by all the Church's faithful.

—John Paul II, *Ordinatio Sacerdotalis*, May 22, 1994

✦

Human words are insufficient to do justice to the mystery which the priesthood involves.

—John Paul II, *Gift and Mystery,* 1996

Last Rites

Inasmuch as [habitual sinners] fell through frailty of the flesh, we bid you succor them with the gift of the viaticum, through the grace of communion, when they start on their way to the Lord.

—St. Siricius, Letter to Bishop Himerius of Tarragona, 385

✦

The anointing is therefore a source of strength for both the soul and the body, but always in order that bodily healing may bring greater union with God through the increase of grace.

—John Paul II, *The Seven Sacraments,* October 1982

IX

SACRED SCRIPTURE

Those genuine and clear [truths] which flow from the very pure fountains of the Scriptures cannot be disturbed by any arguments of misty subtlety.

—St. Simplicius, Letter to Emperor Basil, January 10, 476

✦

The Bible is a stream wherein the elephant may swim and the lamb may wade.

—St. Gregory I the Great, *Sayings of St. Gregory the Great,* c. 595

✦

Learn the heart of God in the words of God, that you may sigh more eagerly for things eternal, that your soul may be kindled with greater longings for heavenly joys.

—St. Gregory I the Great, *Letters,* c. 595

✦

Sacred Scripture is set up as a kind of lantern for us in the night of this life.

—St. Gregory I the Great, *Pastoral Care,* c. 590

✦

Holy Writ is set before the eye of the mind like a kind of mirror, that we may see our inward face in it; for therein we learn the deformities, therein we learn the beauties we possess; there we are made sensible of what progress we are making, there too how far we are from proficiency.

—St. Gregory I the Great, *Moralia on Job*, c. 604

✦

With God . . . we shall arrive at the measure of right faith which the apostles of the truth have extended by means of the slender rope of the Sacred Scriptures.

—Honorius I, Letter to Sergius, Patriarch of Constantinople, 634

✦

God, the Lord almighty, is the only author of both the Old and the New Testaments.

—St. Leo IX, Letter to Peter, Patriarch of Antioch, 1053

✦

It is useful and necessary at all times, in all places, and for every kind of person, to study and to know the spirit, the piety, and the mysteries of Sacred Scripture.

—Clement XI, *Unigenitus*, September 8, 1713

✦

The sense of Holy Scripture can nowhere be found uncorrupt outside the Church, and cannot be expected to be found in writers who, being without the true faith, only know the bark of Sacred Scripture, and never attain the pith.

—Leo XIII, *Providentissimus Deus,* November 18, 1893

✦

You will not find a page in [St. Jerome's] writings which does not show clearly that he, in common with the whole Catholic Church, firmly and consistently held that the Sacred Books—written as they were under the inspiration of the Holy Spirit—have God for their Author, and as such were delivered to the Church.

—Benedict XV, *Spiritus Paraclitus,* September 15, 1920

✦

The word of God reveals the final destiny of men and women and provides a unifying explanation of all that they do in the world.

— John Paul II, *Fides et Ratio,* September 14, 1998

X

THE LIFE OF PRAYER

Be prudent therefore, and watch in prayers.

—St. Peter, First Epistle, 4:7, c. 45

✦

Let us, therefore, approach him in holiness of soul, lifting up to him pure and undefiled hands, loving our gentle and compassionate Father who made us his chosen portion.

—St. Clement I, *Letter to the Corinthians,* c. 95

✦

Let us also intercede for those who are involved in some transgression, that forbearance and humility may be given them, so that they may submit, not to us but to the will of God.

—St. Clement I, *Letter to the Corinthians,* c. 95

✦

We ascend to the heights of contemplation by the steps of the active life.

—St. Gregory I the Great, *Morals,* c. 595

✦

The Divinity never imparts Himself as He is to those that contemplate Him . . . but shows forth His brightness scantily to the blinking eyes of our mind.

—St. Gregory I the Great, *Morals,* c. 595

✦

It is no small labor for the pious individual to guard his own soul.

—St. Gregory VII, Letter to Hermann, Bishop of Metz, March 15, 1081

✦

Nothing has so great a power to obtain grace for us as prayer . . . by which God easily allows Himself to be appeased and to incline to mercy.

—Leo XIII, *Exeunte Jam Anno*, December 25, 1888

✦

For centuries without interruption, from midnight to midnight, the divine psalmody of the inspired canticles is repeated on earth; there is no hour of the day that is not hallowed by its special liturgy; there is no state of human life that has not its part in the thanksgiving, praise, supplication and reparation of this common prayer of the Mystical Body of Christ which is His Church!

—Pius XI, *Caritate Christi,* May 3, 1932

✦

God cannot be honored worthily unless the mind and heart turn to Him in quest of the perfect life.

—Pius XII, *Mediator Dei*, November 20, 1947

✦

When in prayer, the voice repeats those hymns written under the inspiration of the Holy Ghost and extols God's infinite perfections.

—Pius XII, *Mediator Dei*, November 20, 1947

✦

Put aside a little time in the evening especially for praying, for meditating, for reading a page of the Gospel or an episode in the life of some saint. Create a zone of desert and silence for yourself in that way.

—John Paul II, Solitude and Silence Nourish the Spiritual Life, 1998

XI

DISCOVERING THE TRUTH

Lord, to whom shall we go? Thou hast the words of eternal life.

—St. Peter, John 4:69, c. 30

✦

Whatever, therefore, is faultless is defended by the Church Catholic.

—St. Callixtus I, Letter to Bishop Benedict, c. 220

✦

A man will gladly face misrepresentation or even personal danger on behalf of the truth, if he is looking for the blessedness that is to come.

—St. Innocent I, Letter to St. Jerome, 417

✦

Who does not hate, and rage against, and avoid such blind errors, if he have any desire to be saved and seek to offer to the Lord at his coming a right faith?

—Agatho I, Letter to the Third Council of Constantinople, November 15, 680

✦

Man, perhaps, understands one truth perfectly: namely, that nothing is understood perfectly.

—Innocent III, *On the Misery of the Human Condition*, c. 1204

✦

Truth never contradicts truth.

—Leo X, *Apostolici Regiminis*, December 19, 1513

✦

Right reason demonstrates, safeguards and defends the truth of faith, whereas faith frees reason from all errors and through the knowledge of divine things enlightens, strengthens, and perfects it.

—Pius IX, *Qui Pluribus,* 1846

✦

It is perfectly clear and evident, venerable brothers, that the very notion of civilization is a fiction of the brain if it rest not on the abiding principles of truth and the unchanging laws of virtue and justice, and if unfeigned love knit not together the wills of men, and gently control the interchange and the character of their mutual service.

—Pope Leo XIII, *Inscrutabili Dei Consilio,* April 21, 1878

✦

Not in vain did God set the light of reason in the human mind; and so far is the super-added light of faith from extinguishing or lessening the power of the intelligence that it completes it rather, and by adding to its strength renders it capable of greater things.

—Leo XIII, *Aeterni Patris,* August 4, 1879

✦

The Christian faith, reposing on the authority of God, is the unfailing mistress of truth. Whosoever follows it he will be neither enmeshed in the snares of error nor tossed hither and thither on the waves of fluctuating opinion.

—Leo XIII, *Aeterni Patris,* August 4, 1879

✦

Now, it cannot be difficult to find out which is the true religion, if only it be sought with an earnest and unbiased mind; for proofs are abundant and striking.

—Leo XIII, *Immortale Dei*, November 1, 1885

✦

We have, for example, the fulfillment of prophecies, miracles in great numbers, the rapid spread of the faith in the midst of enemies and in face of overwhelming obstacles, the witness of the martyrs, and the like. From all these it is evident that the only true religion is the one established by Jesus Christ Himself, and which He committed to His Church to protect and to propagate.

—Leo XIII, *Immortale Dei,* November 1, 1885

✦

Whosoever departs from the Church wanders far from Christ.

—Leo XIII, *Rerum Novarum*, May 15, 1891

✦

Now the way to reach Christ is not hard to find: it is the Church.

—St. Pius X, *E. Supremi,* October 4, 1903

✦

For the preservation of the moral order . . . religious authority must enter in to enlighten the mind, to direct the will, and to strengthen human frailty by the aid of divine grace.

—Pius XI, *Casti Connubii,* December 31, 1930

✦

Man learns from two books: the universe, for the human study of things created by God; and the Bible, for the study of God's superior will and truth. One belongs to reason, the other to faith. Between them there is no clash.

—Pius XII, Address to the Pontifical Academy of Sciences, December 3, 1939

✦

Truth . . . cannot change from day to day.

—Pius XII, *Humani Generis*, April 12, 1950

✦

Mother and Teacher of all nations—such is the Catholic Church in the mind of her Founder, Jesus Christ. . . . She is "the pillar and ground of the truth" (1 Timothy 3:15).

—John XXIII, *Mater et Magistra,* May 15, 1961

✦

By the natural law every human being has the right to freedom in searching for truth and in expressing and communicating his opinions.

—John XXIII, *Pacem in Terris,* April 11, 1963

✦

The Church's fundamental function in every age and particularly in ours is to direct man's gaze . . . towards the mystery of God.

—John Paul II, *Redemptor Hominis,* March 4, 1979

✦

Truth enlightens man's intelligence and shapes his freedom, leading him to know and love the Lord.

—John Paul II, *Veritatis Splendor*, August 6, 1993

✦

As a result of that mysterious original sin, committed at the prompting of Satan . . . man is constantly tempted to turn his gaze away from the living and true God in order to direct it towards idols, exchanging "the truth about God for a lie" (Romans 1:25).

—John Paul II, *Veritatis Splendor*, August 6, 1993

✦

Man's capacity to know the truth is also darkened, and his will to submit to it is weakened. Thus, giving himself over to relativism and scepticism, he goes off in search of an illusory freedom apart from truth itself.

—John Paul II, *Veritatis Splendor*, August 6, 1993

✦

In all of visible creation, only the human person chooses reflectively. Only the human person can discern between good and evil, and give reasons justifying that discernment. Only human beings can make sacrifices for what is good and true. That is why, throughout Christian history, the martyr remains the paradigm of discipleship: for the martyr lives out the relationship between truth, freedom and goodness in the most radical way.

—John Paul II, Address to American Bishops in Rome, July 1, 1998

✦

Every quest of the human spirit for truth and goodness, and in the last analysis for God, is inspired by the Holy Spirit.

—John Paul II, Seeds of Truth Are Found in Other Religions, September 16, 1998

✦

The knowledge which the Church offers to man has its origin not in any speculation of her own, however sublime, but in the word of God which she has received in faith.

—John Paul II, *Fides et Ratio,* September 14, 1998

✦

Christian Revelation is . . . the ultimate possibility offered by God for the human being to know in all its fullness the seminal plan of love which began with creation.

—John Paul II, *Fides et Ratio,* September 14, 1998

✦

What human reason seeks "without knowing it" (Acts 17:23) can be found only through Christ: what is revealed in him is "the full truth" (John 1:14–16) of everything which was created in him and through him and which therefore in him finds its fulfillment.

—John Paul II, *Fides et Ratio*, September 14, 1998

✦

Revelation clearly proposes certain truths which might never have been discovered by reason unaided, although they are not of themselves inaccessible to reason.

—John Paul II, *Fides et Ratio*, September 14, 1998

✦

Among these truths is the notion of a free and personal God who is the Creator of the world, a truth which has been so crucial for the development of philosophical thinking, especially the philosophy of being.

—John Paul II, *Fides et Ratio,* September 14, 1998

✦

There is also the reality of sin, as it appears in the light of faith, which helps to shape an adequate philosophical formulation of the problem of evil.

—John Paul II, *Fides et Ratio,* September 14, 1998

✦

The notion of the person as a spiritual being is another of faith's specific contributions: the Christian proclamation of human dignity, equality and freedom has undoubtedly influenced modern philosophical thought.

—John Paul II, *Fides et Ratio,* September 14, 1998

XII

THE SEARCH FOR UNITY

Christ established one Church on earth and gave his promise that it would endure until the end of time. He made St. Peter the first shepherd of the Church and commissioned him and his fellow Apostles to carry the faith to the farthest corners of the world. Yet even while the Apostles were still alive, rifts and divisions plagued the Church. Over time, even more serious quarrels arose, so that today we find the one Body of Christ torn by a multitude of denominations.

Origen (185–254) lamented, "Where there are sins, there are also divisions, schisms, heresies, and disputes. Where there is virtue, however, there also are harmony and unity, from which arise the one heart and one soul of all believers."

Even among those denominations that do not accept all that the Catholic Church professes, or that have not kept in communion with the pope, there exist signs of harmony and unity. For example, all Christian denominations initiate new members by baptism. They study the Word of God, cultivate the life of grace, and strive to practice the theological virtues of faith, hope, and charity.

Unique among all the separated Christian churches is the Orthodox Church. In its creed, in its understanding of the Eucharist and the seven sacraments, in its veneration of the Blessed Virgin Mary and the saints, the Orthodox Church is almost in complete agreement with the Catholic Church. The bond of unity between these two sister churches is so profound that, as Pope Paul VI once said, "It lacks little to attain the fullness that would permit a common celebration of the Lord's Eucharist."

Yet even those who have not accepted the Gospel are related to the Church in various ways. Judaism is Christianity's elder brother. St. Paul says that to the Jews "belongeth the adoption as of children, and the glory, and the testament, and the giving of the law, and the service of God, and the promises" (Romans 9:4). All of these things are the shared inheritance of Christians and Jews.

In the same way, the Church rejoices over those points of doctrine that she shares with Islam. Christians and Muslims worship the one living, true, and merciful God. They revere Abraham as their father in faith. And they try to live their lives so as to be prepared when God returns on the dreadful day of judgment.

All humankind has come from a single source; therefore the Church finds common ground even among people who do not know God. At the Second Vatican Council, the Fathers recast in a positive light the ancient maxim, "Outside the Church there is no salvation." In the document *Lumen Gentium,* they wrote that salvation was possible for those who "seek God with a sincere heart, and, moved by grace, try in their actions to do his will as they know it through the dictates of their conscience."

Today as always, the Catholic Church prays and works to bring back its children who have drifted away, to reunite with Christians who have separated themselves from the Catholic communion, and to carry the faith to those who do not know Christ. The ancient Fathers compared the Church to Noah's ark: no matter what storms may roar outside, those within are safe.

◆◆◆

Why do we wrench and tear apart the members of Christ?

—St. Clement I, *Letter to the Corinthians*, c. 95

✦

Imitate the Good Shepherd, Who seeks for the lost sheep and brings it back on His shoulder.

—St. Leo I the Great, *Letter 171*, August 18, 460

✦

In thy zeal for the service of God, aim at winning back to Him, by the prayers of the Church, all those who have in any way strayed from it.

—St. Leo I the Great, *Letter 171*, August 18, 460

✦

We believe and confess one God, although in different ways, and praise and worship Him daily as the Creator of all ages.

—St. Gregory VII, Letter to Anzir, King of Mauritania, 1076

✦

We desire one thing: that the Holy Church, now trampled upon and in confusion and divided into parties, may return to its former unity and splendor.

—St. Gregory VII, *Letter to All the Faithful*, 1082

✦

It is contrary to the Christian religion to force someone into accepting and practicing Christianity if he is always unwilling and totally opposed.

—Innocent III, Letter to Humbert, Archbishop of Arles, 1201

✦

How, indeed, is the Greek Church to be brought back into ecclesiastical union and to a devotion for the Apostolic See when she has been beset with so many afflictions and persecutions that she sees in the Latins only an example of perdition and the works of darkness, so that she now, and with reason, detests the Latins more than dogs?

—Innocent III, Letter to Cardinal Peter, Papal Legate, July 12, 1204

✦

Let it never happen that the children of the Catholic Church be in any way at enmity with those who are not joined to them by the bonds of the same faith and love.

—Pius IX, Letter to the Bishops of Italy, 1863

✦

The true union between Christians is that which Jesus Christ, the Author of the Church, instituted and desired, and which consists in a unity of faith and a unity of government.

—Leo XIII, *Praeclara Gratulationis Publicae*, June 20, 1894

✦

Catholics are in duty bound to practical political, civic and social tolerance with respect to the faithful of other denominations.

—Pius XII, Address to Members of the Rota, October 6, 1946

✦

The Catholic Church is a stranger to no people on earth, much less hostile to any.

—Pius XII, *Ad Apostolorum Principis*, June 29, 1958

✦

"An example of perdition and the works of darkness": Innocent III Condemns the Sack of Constantinople

{*One of the most shameful episodes of the Middle Ages was the sack of Constantinople by the armies of the Fourth Crusade. Diverted by greed from their sworn purpose of liberating the Holy Land from the Saracens, the Crusaders attacked the city on April 9, 1204. Three days later they breached the walls. An orgy of rape, murder, larceny, and sacrilege followed, from which the Byzantine Empire never recovered. When word of the outrage reached Rome, Pope Innocent III sent an angry letter, dated July 12, 1204, to his Papal Legate, Cardinal Peter of St. Marcellus. The Pope was furious that Peter had sanctioned the attack on Constantinople, not only because it left the Holy Land defenseless, but also because it did irreparable harm to the longed-for reunion between the Catholic and Orthodox Churches.*}

✦

We were not a little astonished and disturbed to hear that you and our beloved son, the Cardinal Priest of the Title of St. Praxida and Legate of the Apostolic See, in fear of the looming perils of the Holy Land, have left the province of Jerusalem (which, at this point is in such great need) and that you have gone by ship to Constantinople. And now we see that what we dreaded has occurred and what we feared has come to pass. . . .

For you, who ought to have looked for help for the Holy Land, you who should have stirred up others, both by word and by example, to assist the Holy Land—on your own initiative you sailed to Greece, bringing in your footsteps not

continued

only the pilgrims, but even the natives of the Holy Land who came to Constantinople, following our venerable brother, the Archbishop of Tyre. When you had deserted it, the Holy Land remained destitute of men, void of strength. Because of you, its last state was worse than the first, for all its friends deserted with you; nor was there any admirer to console it. . . . We ourselves were not a little agitated and, with reason, we acted against you, since you had fallen in with this counsel and because you had deserted the Land which the Lord consecrated by his presence, the land in which our King marvelously performed the mystery of our redemption. . . .

It was your duty to attend to the business of your legation and to give careful consideration, not to the capture of the Empire of Constantinople, but rather to the defense of what is left of the Holy Land and, with the Lord's leave, the restoration of what has been lost. We made you our representative and we sent you to gain, not temporal, but rather eternal riches. And for this purpose, our brethren provided adequately for your needs.

We have just heard and discovered from your letters that you have absolved from their pilgrimage vows and their crusading obligations all the Crusaders who have remained to defend Constantinople from last March to the present. It is impossible not to be moved against you, for you neither should nor could give any such absolution.

Whoever suggested such a thing to you and how did they ever lead your mind astray? . . .

How, indeed, is the Greek church to be brought back into ecclesiastical union and to a devotion for the Apostolic See when she has been beset with so many afflictions and persecutions that she sees in the Latins only an example of perdition and the works of darkness, so that she now, and with reason, detests the Latins more than dogs? As for those who were supposed to be seeking the ends of Jesus Christ, not their own ends, whose swords, which they were supposed to use against the pagans, are now dripping with Christian blood—they have spared neither age nor sex. They have committed incest, adultery, and fornication before the eyes of men. They have exposed both matrons and virgins, even those dedicated to God, to the sordid lusts of boys. Not satisfied with breaking open the imperial treasury and plundering the goods of princes and lesser men, they also laid their hands on the treasures of the churches and, what is more serious, on their very possessions. They have even ripped silver plates from the altars and have hacked them to pieces among themselves. They violated the holy places and have carried off crosses and relics.

Furthermore, under what guise can we call upon the other Western peoples for aid to the Holy Land and assistance to the Empire of Constantinople? When the Crusaders, having given up the proposed pilgrimage, return absolved to their homes; when those who plundered the aforesaid Empire turn back and come home with their spoils, free of guilt; will not people then suspect that these things have happened, not because of the crime involved, but because of your deed? Let the Lord's word not be stifled in your mouth. Be not like a dumb dog, unable to bark. Rather, let them speak these things publicly, let them protest before everyone, so that the more they rebuke you before God and on God's account, the more they will find you simply negligent.

The life of each of the sons of God is joined, in Christ and through Christ, to the lives of all his brother Christians by a wonderful link in the supernatural oneness of the mystical Body of Christ.

—Paul VI, *Indulgentiarum Doctrina*, January 1, 1967

✦

We are all united in this progress toward God.

—Paul VI, *Populorum Progressio,* March 26, 1967

✦

The Fathers of the Church rightly saw in the various religions as it were so many reflections of the one truth, seeds of the Word, attesting that, though the routes taken may be different, there is but a single goal to which is directed the deepest aspiration of the human spirit as expressed in its quest for God and . . . the full meaning of human life.

—John Paul II, *Redemptor Hominis*, March 4, 1979

✦

All of us who are Christ's followers must therefore meet and unite around Him.

—John Paul II, *Redemptor Hominis*, March 4, 1979

✦

Christ is thus the fulfillment of the yearning of all the world's religions and, as such, he is their sole and definitive completion.

—John Paul II, *Tertio Mellennio Adveniente,* November 14, 1994

✦

We proceed along the road leading to the conversion of hearts guided by love which is directed to God and, at the same time, to all our brothers and sisters, including those not in full communion with us.

—John Paul II, *Ut Unum Sint,* May 25, 1995

✦

Full communion of course will have to come about through the acceptance of the whole truth into which the Holy Spirit guides Christ's disciples. Hence all forms of reductionism or facile "agreement" must be absolutely avoided. Serious questions must be resolved, for if not, they will reappear at another time, either in the same terms or in a different guise.

—John Paul II, *Ut Unum Sint*, May 25, 1995

✦

Christ is sending us out together, so that we may jointly bear witness to him. Thus we cannot remain separated! We must walk together, because this is Our Lord's will.

—John Paul II, *We Cannot Remain Separated,* June 29, 1995

XIII

FAITH

Lord, to whom shall we go? Thou hast the words of eternal life.

—St. Peter, John 6:69, c. 30

✦

Lord, thou knowest all things. Thou knowest that I love thee.

—St. Peter, John 21:17, c. 30

✦

May Almighty God and His Son, our Lord and Savior Jesus Christ, grant you His grace forever in recompense for your marvelous faith.

—St. Julius I, Letter to the Christians of Alexandria, 343

✦

Even if I am alone, the word of faith is not weakened for that.

—Liberius, Interview with Emperor Constantius, 355

✦

Do you abide on firm ground, strong in the faith and immovable.

—St. Damasus, Letter to the Bishops of the East, 378

✦

If the work of God could be comprehended by reason, it would no longer be wonderful, and faith would have no merit if reason provided proof.

—St. Gregory I the Great, *Homilies on the Gospels*, c. 590

✦

Faith is the first of all virtues.

—St. Nicholas I, Response to the Questions of the Bulgars, 866.

✦

Faith gives life to a just man.

—Sylvester II, Letter to Arnulf, c. 1000

✦

The most important and absolutely necessary thing in the Church of God is faith.

—Pius II, *De Summo Pontifice*, 1460

✦

No graces are granted except through faith. Faith is the first grace and the source of all others.

—Clement XI, *Unigenitus*, September 8, 1713

✦

O my God, I believe in You; do You strengthen my faith.

—Clement XI, *A Universal Prayer*, c. 1715

✦

Though faith is above reason, there can never be found a real contradiction or disagreement between them.

—Pius IX, *Qui Pluribus*, 1846

✦

Our holy religion is not invented by human reason but mercifully revealed by God to men.

—Pius IX, *Qui Pluribus*, 1846

✦

[Faith] has overthrown the fallacy of idols and dissipated the darkness of errors; it has triumphed over enemies of every kind.

—Pius IX, *Qui Pluribus,* 1846

✦

There is nothing more certain than our faith, nothing safer, nothing more holy, nothing that rests on firmer principles.

—Pius IX, *Qui Pluribus*, 1846

✦

Supernatural force has never during the flight of ages been found wanting in the Church, nor have Christ's promises failed.

—St. Pius X, *Jucunda Sane*, March 12, 1904

✦

Belief in God is the unshaken foundation of all social order and of all responsible action on earth.

—Pius XI, *Caritate Christi Compulsi*, May 3, 1932

✦

The future belongs to believers and not to skeptics and doubters. The future belongs to those who love, not to those who hate.

—Pius XII, Address to the College of Cardinals, June 2, 1947

✦

By faith in Jesus, "the Author of life," life which lies abandoned and cries out for help regains self-esteem and dignity.

—John Paul II, *Evangelium Vitae*, March 25, 1995

✦

In matters of faith, compromise is in contradiction with God who is Truth.

—John Paul II, *Ut Unum Sint,* May 25, 1995

✦

Our vision of the face of God is always fragmentary and impaired by the limits of our understanding. Faith alone makes it possible to penetrate the mystery in a way that allows us to understand it coherently.

—John Paul II, *Fides et Ratio,* September 14, 1998

✦

Just as grace builds on nature and brings it to fulfillment, so faith builds upon and perfects reason.

—John Paul II, *Fides et Ratio,* September 14, 1998.

XIV

HOPE

With this hope, therefore, let our souls be bound to him who is faithful in his promises and righteous in his judgments.

—St. Clement I, *Letter to the Corinthians,* c. 95

✦

The cross of Christ is the true ground and chief cause of Christian hope.

—St. Leo I, Sermon 56, c. 463

✦

Art thou righteous? Then fear lest thou fall. Art thou a sinner? Then believe in His mercy, that thou mayest rise.

—St. Gregory I the Great, *Homilies on the Gospels*, c. 595

✦

Yet we do not despair nor lose heart, because we put our trust not in ourselves but in Him who works in us.

—St. Leo I the Great, Sermon 3, 461

✦

All my hopes are in You; do You secure them.

—Clement XI, *A Universal Prayer*, c. 1715

✦

✦

This era in which we live is in the grip of deadly errors; it is torn by deep disorders. But it is also an era which offers to those who work with the Church immense possibilities in the field of the apostolate. And therein lies our hope.

—John XXIII, *Mater et Magistra*, May 15, 1961

XV

CHARITY

Who can express the bond of the charity of God? Who can express the splendor of its beauty?

—St. Clement I, *Letter to the Corinthians*, c. 95

✦

He that hath abundance, let him quicken himself to mercy and generosity; he that hath art and skill, let him do his best to share the use and the utility thereof with his neighbor.

—St. Gregory I the Great, *Homilies on the Gospels*, c. 590

✦

What is it you are giving, and to whom are you giving? By your generosity you are, after all, merely giving a little to Him who has freely given you all you have. He does not receive it gratis, but increases the offering. He recompenses it in the future.

—Sylvester II, Appeal for the Holy Land, c. 1000

✦

The perfection of Christian life consists principally and essentially in charity.

—John XXII, *Ad Conditorem*, 1322

✦

God rewards nothing but charity; for charity alone honors God.

—Clement XI, *Unigenitus,* September 8, 1713

✦

If a family perchance is in such extreme difficulty and is so completely without plans that it is entirely unable to help itself, it is right that the distress be remedied by public aid, for each individual family is a part of the community.

—Leo XIII, *Rerum Novarum,* May 15, 1891

✦

No human devices can ever be found to supplant Christian charity, which gives itself entirely for the benefit of others.

—Leo XIII, *Rerum Novarum,* May 15, 1891

✦

As charity towards God has grown cold, the mutual charity of men among themselves has likewise cooled.

—Leo XIII, *Mira Caritatis,* May 28, 1902

✦

Charity will never be true charity unless it takes justice into constant account.

—Pius XI, *Divini Redemptoris*, March 19, 1937

✦

Today the peoples in hunger are making a dramatic appeal to the peoples blessed with abundance. The Church shudders at this cry of anguish and calls each one to give a loving response of charity to this brother's cry for help.

—Paul VI, *Populorum Progressio*, March 26, 1967

✦

Love, when it is genuine, is all-embracing, stable and lasting, an irresistible spur to all forms of heroism.

—Paul VI, *Sacerdotalis Caelibatus*,
June 24, 1967

XVI

GOOD WORKS

Silver and gold I have none; but what I have, I give thee: In the name of Jesus Christ of Nazareth, arise and walk.

—St. Peter, Acts of the Apostles 3:6, c. 30

✦

By doing well you may put to silence the ignorance of foolish men.

—St. Peter, First Epistle 2:15, c. 45

✦

All the saints have been adorned with good works.

—St. Clement I, *Letter to the Corinthians,* c. 95

✦

Let us clothe ourselves with concord and humility, ever exercising self-control, standing far off from all whispering and evil-speaking, being justified by our works, and not our words.

—St. Clement I, *Letter to the Corinthians*, c. 95

✦

Let the wise display his wisdom not in words but in good works.

—St. Clement I, *Letter to the Corinthians*, c. 95

✦

What shall we do, brothers? Shall we idly abstain from doing good, and forsake love?

—St. Clement I, *Letter to the Corinthians*, c. 95

✦

So, just as your body is visible, let your spirit be apparent in your good works.

—St. Soter, *To the Corinthians*, c. 170

✦

The expectation of receiving thanks must not creep into their action, for the desire of transitory praise will extinguish the light of their giving.

—St. Gregory I the Great, *Pastoral Care*, c. 590

✦

Be not anxious about what you have, but about what you are.

—St. Gregory I the Great, *Homilies on the Gospels*, c. 595

✦

Be not surprised, beloved brethren, if the world hates you; for we ourselves provoke the world against us by opposing its desires and condemning its works.

—St. Gregory VII, *Letter to All the Faithful*, 1082

✦

The grace of Jesus Christ, which is the efficacious principle of every kind of good, is necessary for every good work; without it, not only is nothing done, but nothing can be done.

—Clement XI, *Unigenitus,* September 8, 1713

✦

A well-spent life is the only passport to heaven.

—Leo XIII, *Immortale Dei*, November 1, 1885

✦

Nothing emboldens the wicked so greatly as the lack of courage on the part of the good.

—Leo XIII, *Sapientiae Christianae,* January 10, 1890

✦

No one is so rich that he does not need another's help; no one so poor as not to be useful in some way to his fellow man.

—Leo XIII, *Graves de Communi*, January 18, 1901

✦

History bears witness that the virtues of the Christian life have flourished best wherever the frequent reception of the Eucharist has most prevailed.

—Leo XIII, *Mira Caritatis*, May 28, 1902

✦

The Sacred Scriptures and the Fathers of the Church constantly declare in the most explicit language that the rich are bound by a very grave precept to practice almsgiving, beneficence, and munificence.

—Pius XI, *Quadragesimo Anno*, May 15, 1931

✦

Through [the Church] the work and sufferings of redemption are continued throughout human history.

—Paul VI, *Credo of the People of God,* June 30, 1968

✦

Just as Mary visited Elizabeth, so you too are called to "visit" the needs of the poor, the hungry, the homeless, those who are alone or ill; for example, those suffering from AIDS.

—John Paul II, Homily in Central Park, October 7, 1995

XVII

OBEDIENCE

We ought to obey God rather than men.

—St. Peter, Acts of the Apostles 5:29, c. 30

✦

Since the long-enduring patience of God summons you to improvement, we hope that with increase of understanding, your heart and mind may be turned to obey the commands of God.

—St. Gregory VII, Letter to Emperor Henry IV, December 1075

✦

It would have been becoming to you, since you confess yourself to be a son of the Church, to give more respectful attention to the master of the Church, that is, to Peter, prince of the Apostles.

—St. Gregory VII, Letter to Emperor Henry IV, January 8, 1076

✦

If a man says he cannot be bound by the ban of the Church, it is evident that he could not be loosed by its authority, and he who shamelessly denies this cuts himself off absolutely from Christ.

—St. Gregory VII, Letter to Hermann, Bishop of Metz, August 25, 1076

✦

Return to submission to Mother Church, a submission as honorable as it is salutary, and know that we have here below no keener desire than that of your salvation.

—Benedict XI, Letter to Philip IV of France, April 5, 1384

✦

Obedience is not servitude of man to man, but submission to the will of God, Who governs through the medium of men.

—Leo XIII, *Immortale Dei,* November 1, 1885

✦

When anything is commanded which is plainly at variance with the will of God . . . it is not right to obey.

—Leo XIII, *Libertas Praestantissimum*, June 20, 1888

✦

There exists no authority except from God.

—Pius XII, Address to the Women of Italian Catholic Action, October 26, 1941

✦

Whereas the disobedience of Adam had ruined and marred God's plan for human life and introduced death into the world, the redemptive obedience of Christ is the source of grace poured out upon the human race, opening wide to everyone the gates of the kingdom of life.

—John Paul II, *Evangelium Vitae*, March 25, 1995

✦

In the case of an intrinsically unjust law, such as a law permitting abortion or euthanasia, it is therefore never licit to obey it.

—John Paul II, *Evangelium Vitae*, March 25, 1995

XVIII

PATIENCE

The true religion has shone forth with greater splendor the more it has been oppressed.

—St. Symmachus, Letter to Emperor Anastasius, c. 506

✦

We, then, willingly bear the insults addressed to us personally, more especially when they are caused by our ardor for justice, and when their authors are the foes of that justice.

—St. Nicholas I, Letter to Emperor Michael III, 863

✦

If you shall be our companions in sorrow, you shall also, with God's help, be partners in our joy.

—St. Gregory VII, Letter to the Bishops of Southern Italy, July 21, 1080

✦

If the Lord wishes that other persecutions should be suffered, the Church feels no alarm; on the contrary, persecutions purify her and confer upon her fresh force and a new beauty.

—Pius IX, *The Deeds and Sayings of Pius IX*, 1874

✦

It is often very difficult for poor human nature, oppressed by the weight of sickness . . . to be resigned, to go on believing that God loves it still when He lets it suffer so.

—Pius XII, Radio Address to the Sick, November 21, 1949

XIX

PEACE

Let us unite with those who devoutly practice peace, and not with those who hypocritically wish for peace.

—St. Clement I, *Letter to the Corinthians*, c. 95

✦

Provide that our days be spent in your peace, save us from everlasting damnation, and cause us to be numbered in the flock you have chosen.

—St. Gregory I the Great, Prayer added to the Canon of the Mass, c. 595

✦

The desire for peace is certainly harbored in every breast, and there is no one who does not ardently invoke it.

—St. Pius X, *E Supremi,* October 4, 1903

✦

To want peace without God is an absurdity, seeing that where God is absent thence too justice flies, and when justice is taken away it is vain to cherish the hope of peace.

—St. Pius X, *E Supremi,* October 4, 1903

✦

Our Lord Jesus Christ came down from Heaven for the very purpose of restoring amongst men the Kingdom of Peace, which the envy of the devil had destroyed, and it was His will that it should rest on no other foundation than that of brotherly love.

—Benedict XV, *Ad Beatissimi Apostolorum,* November 1, 1914

✦

If the desire for worldly possessions were kept within bounds and the place of honor in our affections given to the things of the spirit, which place undoubtedly they deserve, the peace of Christ would follow immediately.

—Pius XI, *Ubi Arcano Dei Consilio,* December 23, 1922

✦

We do not need a peace that will consist merely in acts of external or formal courtesy, but a peace which will penetrate the souls of men and which will unite, heal, and reopen their hearts to that mutual affection which is born of brotherly love.

—Pius XI, *Ubi Arcano Dei Consilio,* December 23, 1922

✦

Nothing is lost by peace; everything may be lost by war.

—Pius XII, Radio Message, August 24, 1939

✦

Had God, with his inscrutable and always just advice on world government, only granted us the power to find some way of checking the bloody events!

—Pius XII, Address to the Sacred College of Cardinals, June 2, 1940

✦

Salvation and justice are not to be found in revolution, but in evolution through concord.

—Pius XII, Address to Workers from the Dioceses of Italy, June 13, 1943

✦

Violence has always achieved only destruction, not construction; the kindling of passions, not their pacification; the accumulation of hate and ruin, not the reconciliation of the contending parties. And it has reduced men and parties to the difficult task of rebuilding, after sad experience, on the ruins of discord.

—Pius XII, Address to Workers from the Dioceses of Italy, June 13, 1943

✦

To serve the cause of peace is to serve justice. To serve the cause of peace is to serve the interests of the people, especially the lowly and the dispossessed.

—Pius XII, *Now Is the Time for Action*, September 7, 1947

✦

Peace worthy of the name must be founded on the principles of charity and justice which He taught who is the Prince of Peace, and who adopted this title as a kind of royal standard for Himself.

—Pius XII, *Ad Apostolorum Principis,* June 29, 1958

✦

True peace is that which the Church desires to be established: one that is stable, just, fair, and founded on right order; one which binds all together—citizens, families, and peoples—by the firm ties of the rights of the Supreme Lawgiver, and by the bonds of mutual fraternal love and cooperation.

—Pius XII, *Ad Apostolorum Principis,* June 29, 1958

✦

Peace on earth, which all men of every era have most eagerly yearned for, can be firmly established only if the order laid down by God be dutifully observed.

—John XXIII, *Pacem in Terris*, April 11, 1963

✦

Justice, then, right reason and consideration for human dignity and life urgently demand that the arms race should cease; that the stockpiles which exist in various countries should be reduced equally and simultaneously by the parties concerned; that nuclear weapons should be banned; and finally that all come to an agreement on a fitting program of disarmament, employing mutual and effective controls.

—John XXIII, *Pacem in Terris*, April 11, 1963

✦

Is there anyone who does not ardently yearn to see dangers of war banished, to see peace preserved and daily more firmly established?

—John XXIII, *Pacem in Terris*, April 11, 1963

✦

Peace will be but an empty-sounding word unless it is founded on . . . truth, built according to justice, vivified and integrated by charity, and put into practice in freedom.

—John XXIII, *Pacem in Terris*, April 11, 1963

✦

Peace comes down to respect for man's inviolable rights . . . while war springs from the violation of these rights and brings with it still graver violations of them.

—John Paul II, *Redemptor Hominis*, March 4, 1979

✦

Peace which is not built upon the values of the dignity of every individual and of solidarity between all people frequently proves to be illusory.

—John Paul II, *Evangelium Vitae,* March 25, 1995

✦

No form of violence can settle conflicts between individuals or nations, for violence begets violence.

—John Paul II, Address on 50th Anniversary of Pax Christi Movement,
May 29, 1995

✦

Neither the reduction in the number of weapons, disarmament, nor the absence of war lead immediately to peace. It is essential to create a culture of life and a culture of peace.

—John Paul II, Address on the 50th Anniversary of the Pax Christi Movement,
May 29, 1995

XX

SIN, REPENTANCE, AND FORGIVENESS

Depart from me, for I am a sinful man, O Lord.

—St. Peter, Luke 5:8, c. 30

✦

Be penitent, therefore, and be converted, that your sins may be blotted out.

—St. Peter, Acts of the Apostles 3:19, c. 30

✦

You were not redeemed with corruptible things as gold and silver . . . but with the precious blood of Christ, as of a lamb unspotted and undefiled.

—St. Peter, First Epistle 1:18–19, c. 45

✦

Be sober and watch: because your adversary the devil, as a roaring lion, goeth about seeking whom he may devour.

—St. Peter, First Epistle 5:8, c. 45

✦

Learn to submit yourselves, laying aside the arrogant and proud stubbornness of your tongue.

—St. Clement, *Letter to the Corinthians*, c. 95

✦

For I myself am altogether sinful and have not yet escaped from temptation but am still beset by the wiles of the devil. Nevertheless I strive to follow after righteousness, that I may have strength at least to approach it, fearing the judgment that is to come.

—St. Soter, *To the Corinthians,* c. 170

✦

Dost thou not know that the goodness of God leadeth thee to repentance?

—St. Callixtus I, Letter to the Bishops of Gaul, c. 220

✦

Repentance wipes out the guilt of ignorance.

—Liberius, Letter to the Bishops of Italy, 359

✦

Under the eye of the Master, Christ, the conscience, having been purged, will find rest in the haven of peace.

—St. Innocent I, Letter to St. John Chrysostom, c. 417

✦

The soul that thirsts for God is first sorry in his heart from fear, and then from love.

—St. Gregory I the Great, *Dialogues,* c. 590

✦

A sin that is not quickly blotted out by repentance, is both a sin and a cause of sin.

—St. Gregory I the Great, *Homily 11,* c. 590

✦

Why do those whose strength is in iniquity take pride in their ill-doing?

—St. Nicholas I, Letter to Emperor Michael III, 863

✦

If anyone desires to perform a proper penance, he must needs go back to the origins of his faith and with watchful care keep the promise made at his baptism, namely, to renounce the Devil and all his works and to believe in God, that is, to have the right idea of him, and to obey his commandments.

—St. Gregory VII, Letter to the Bishops and Barons of Brittany, November 25, 1079

✦

Pride inflates man; envy consumes him; avarice makes him restless; anger rekindles his passions; gluttony makes him ill; comfort destroys him; lies imprison him; murder defiles him . . . the very pleasures of sin become the instruments of punishment in the hands of God.

—Innocent III, *On the Misery of the Human Condition,* c. 1204

✦

What else remains for the soul that has lost God and His grace except sin and the consequences of sin, a proud poverty and a slothful indigence, that is, a general impotence for labor, for prayer, and for every good work?

—Clement XI, *Unigenitus,* September 8, 1713

✦

Howsoever remote from salvation an obstinate sinner is, when Jesus presents Himself to be seen by him in the salutary light of His grace, the sinner is forced to surrender himself, to have recourse to Him, and to humble himself, and to adore his Savior.

—Clement XI, *Unigenitus,* September 8, 1713

✦

Give me strength, O God, to expiate my offenses, to overcome my temptations, to subdue my passions, and to acquire the virtues proper to my state.

—Clement XI, *A Universal Prayer,* c. 1715

✦

Rouse your enthusiasm at the announcement of so great a gift offered you. Undertake the task that can save your souls with great eagerness and fervor.

—Benedict XIV, *Peregrinantes,* May 5, 1749

✦

Let not the comforts of home hold you back; let not the labor of the journey frighten you. Weigh the spiritual gift by the standards of the Christian faith and do not permit the eagerness of worldly men for earthly treasure to surpass the desire of the faithful for heavenly treasures.

—Benedict XIV, *Peregrinantes,* May 5, 1749

✦

Far from Us, Venerable Brethren, be the idea of daring to set limits to the divine mercy, which is infinite; far also from Us to want to penetrate the secret plans and judgments of God which are "like the great deep" (Psalm 36:6), impenetrable to human thought.

—Pius IX, *Allocution to the Sacred College of Cardinals*, 1854

✦

Since it is in the very nature of man to follow the guide of reason in his actions, if his intellect sins at all, his will soon follows; and thus it happens that false opinions, whose seat is in the understanding, influence human actions and pervert them.

—Leo XIII, *Aeterni Patris*, August 4, 1879

✦

The evil consequences of sin are hard, trying, and bitter to bear, and will necessarily accompany men even to the end of life.

—Leo XIII, *Rerum Novarum*, May 15, 1891

✦

Since our hearts, disturbed as they are at times by the lower appetites, do not always respond to motives of love, it is also extremely helpful to let consideration and contemplation of the justice of God provoke us on occasion to salutary fear, and guide us thence to Christian humility, repentance and amendment.

—Pius XII, *Mediator Dei*, November 20, 1947

✦

Certainly, no one was better fitted to make satisfaction to Almighty God for all the sins of men than was Christ. . . . He daily offers Himself upon our altars for our redemption, that we may be rescued from eternal damnation and admitted into the company of the elect.

—Pius XII, *Mediator Dei*, November 20, 1947

✦

Nothing is better able to restrain the movements of the soul, better able to subject to right reason the natural appetites, than penance.

—Pius XII, Homily on the Canonization of St. Mariana de Jesus de Paredes, July 9, 1950

✦

When man loses the consciousness of his personal dignity and of right measure and equilibrium in his activity, when spiritual, religious, supernatural and eternal values no longer render man happy and are in fact not even understood, it is inevitable that greed and avarice should begin to assert their sway, and that the cult of material and mechanical power should replace the worship of God.

—Pius XII, Allocution to the Sacred College of Cardinals, November 2, 1950

✦

We must watch particularly over the movements of our passions and of our senses, and so control them by voluntary discipline in our lives and by bodily mortification that we render them obedient to right reason and God's law.

—Pius XII, *Sacra Virginitas,* March 25, 1954

✦

There is, alas, a spirit of hedonism abroad today which beguiles men into thinking that life is nothing more than the quest for pleasure and the satisfaction of human passions. This attitude is disastrous.

—John XXIII, *Mater et Magistra,* May 15, 1961

✦

The Gospels and the whole ascetic tradition of the Church require a sense of mortification and penance which assures the rule of the spirit over the flesh, and offers an efficacious means of expiating the punishment due to sin, from which no one, except Jesus Christ and His Immaculate Mother, is exempt.

—John XXIII, *Mater et Magistra,* May 15, 1961

✦

Every sin brings with it a disturbance of the universal order, which God arranged in unspeakable wisdom and infinite love.

—Paul VI, *Indulgentiarum Doctrina,* January 1, 1967

✦

[The Church] knows men's weaknesses, has compassion on the crowd, receives sinners; but she cannot renounce the teaching of the law which is, in reality, that law proper to a human life restored to its original truth and conducted by the spirit of God.

—Paul VI, *Humanae Vitae,* July 25, 1968

✦

We can presume that [the Devil's] sinister action is at work where the denial of God becomes radical, subtle and absurd; where lies become powerful and hypocritical in the face of evident truth; where love is smothered by cold, cruel selfishness; where Christ's name is attacked with conscious, rebellious hatred; where the spirit of the Gospel is watered down and rejected; where despair is affirmed as the last word.

—Paul VI, *Confronting the Devil's Power,* November 15, 1972

✦

As long as time lasts, the struggle between good and evil continues even in the human heart itself.

—John Paul II, *Centisimus Annus,* May 1, 1991

✦

All the conditioning and efforts to enforce silence fail to stifle the voice of the Lord echoing in the conscience of every individual.

—John Paul II, *Evangelium Vitae,* March 25, 1995

✦

No circumstance, no purpose, no law whatsoever can ever make licit an act which is intrinsically illicit, since it is contrary to the Law of God which is written in every human heart, knowable by reason itself, and proclaimed by the Church.

—John Paul II, *Evangelium Vitae,* March 25, 1995

XXI

THE PRIMACY OF THE POPES

"And I say to thee: That thou art Peter; and upon this rock I will build my church, and the gates of hell shall not prevail against it. And I will give to thee the keys of the kingdom of heaven. And whatsoever thou shalt bind upon earth, it shall be bound also in heaven: and whatsoever thou shalt loose on earth, it shall be loosed also in heaven" [Matthew 16:18–19].

"When therefore they had dined, Jesus saith to Simon Peter: Simon, son of John, lovest thou me more than these? He saith to him: Yea, Lord, thou knowest that I love thee. He saith to him: Feed my lambs. He saith to him again: Simon, son of John, lovest thou me? He saith to him: Yea, Lord, thou knowest that I love thee. He saith to him: Feed my lambs. He said to him the third time: Simon, son of John, lovest thou me? Peter was grieved, because he had said to him the third time: Lovest thou me? And he said to him: Lord, thou knowest all things: thou knowest that I love thee. He said to him: Feed my sheep" [John 21:15–17].

And the Lord said: Simon, Simon, behold Satan hath desired to have you, that he may sift you as wheat. But I have prayed for thee, that thy faith fail not: and thou, being once converted, confirm thy brethren" [Luke 22:31–32].

These three passages of the Gospels are the foundation upon which the doctrine of the Papacy is built. The first passage, of course, is the most famous, the one most frequently quoted to support the faith that Christ gave authority over the Church to St. Peter and his successors. (Visitors to Rome will find this proof-text inscribed in letters nearly six feet high around the interior of the great dome of St. Peter's in the Vatican.)

Rome is the city of the popes because it was in Rome that St. Peter taught the Gospel and it was in Rome that he was martyred about A.D. 67 during Nero's persecution of the Christians. The oldest surving document which suggests that the Bishop of Rome exercised authority over the churches is St. Clement I's *Letter to the Corinthians,* written around the year 95. Clement wrote to heal the dissensions that had divided the Christians of Corinth into rancorous camps. If St. John, who is believed to have still been alive at this time, had acted to resolve the conflict, it would come to us as no surprise, because he was one of the Twelve Apostles. The fact that it is the fourth bishop of Rome who steps in suggests that his authority was recognized by Christians outside the city of Rome. Furthermore, we know that the letter was revered by subsequent generations of Christians: seventy years later, St. Dionysius, Bishop of Corinth, reports that Clement's letter is still being read in the city's churches.

St. Clement's letter is just one example of the preeminence the Church of Rome enjoyed among the other churches. In their writings, St. Ignatius of Antioch (died c. 110), St. Ireneaus of Lyon (c. 130–200), Tertullian (c. 166–220), and the St. Cyprian of Carthage (c. 200–258) demonstrate that they recognized the spiritual authority of Rome. For their part, the surviving documents written by early popes such as St. Soter (died c. 174), St. Callixtus (died 222), St. Fabian (died 250), and St. Cornelius (died 253) convey a profound sense of responsibility for the Church throughout the Roman Empire, not just for the Christians directly under their jurisdiction in Rome. By the third century, according to the historian Eamon Duffy, "The church at Rome was an acknowledged point of refer-

> ## "*It is your duty to come to Rome: therefore come.*"
>
> {*In 1309, Pope Clement V took up residence in Avignon in the south of France. Given the political upheavals in Italy at the time, it seemed like a judicious, temporary solution. In fact, the stay lasted much longer than Clement probably expected. Sixty-three years and six popes later, the Papacy was still in Avignon, and it was firmly under the influence of the French king. In the summer of 1376, St. Catherine of Siena, a twenty-nine-year-old mystic, traveled to Avignon to convince Pope Gregory XI to return to Rome. Gregory wanted to go, but he was hesitant. His advisers frightened the Pope with tales of cutthroats and poisoners who would lie in wait for him along his way to Rome. Catherine found it necessary to speak forcefully to the Holy Father.*}
>
> ✦
>
> I will pray the good and sweet Jesus to despoil you of all servile fear and to leave in you only a holy fear. May the fire of charity burn in you so that you will not be able to hear the
>
> *continued*

ence for Christians throughout the Mediterranean world, and might even function as a court of appeal" to resolve matters of doctrine and religious discipline.

The authority the popes have exercised from the beginning is known as "the power of the keys," an allusion to the keys to the kingdom of heaven Christ conferred upon St. Peter. By virtue of the keys, the pope, St. Peter's successor, governs the Church. Also part of the pope's commission is the power to "bind and to loose," by which Christ granted him the power to absolve sins, define Catholic doctrine, and set policy regarding Catholic religious practice. Finally, Christ instructed St. Peter, "Feed my lambs . . . feed voices of the incarnate devils who, from what I learn, wish to place obstacles to your return by suggesting, in order to frighten you, that you will be surrendering yourself to certain death. I say to you in the name of Christ crucified, most sweet and holy Father, that you have no cause for fear. Come in all confidence and trust in Christ, sweet Jesus. If you do your duty, God will protect you and no one can prevail against you.

Courage, Father; be a man! I say to you that you have nothing to fear. But if you neglect to do your duty, then indeed you have cause to fear. It is your duty to come to Rome; therefore come. . . . And if anyone tries to prevent you, then say boldly what Christ said to St. Peter, who out of the tenderness of his love wished Him to avoid the Passion: "Get thee behind me, Satan!"

. . . So do you likewise, dearest Father. Imitate Him whose Vicar you are and say to all those around you: "Though I should lose my life a thousand times, yet will I do the will of my Father!"

my sheep," an attractive metaphor for a solemn responsibility: to safeguard the spiritual formation of the Catholic faithful by transmitting the truths Christ taught without compromise.

The pope, then, exercises a dual ministry. He is "Supreme Pontiff"—which means High Priest—but he is also "the servant of the servants of God." He must speak the truth with authority and correct error when necessary, but he is also obliged to show compassion. Because the popes are human, their personal weaknesses will have an effect on how well they exercise their office, yet Christ promised to preserve St. Peter's successors from ever promoting false doctrine. As St. Gregory of Nazianzen observed in the fourth century: "Regarding the faith . . . Rome has kept a straight course from of old, and still does so, uniting the whole West by sound teaching, as is just, since she presides over all and guards the universal divine harmony."

✦ ✦ ✦

If certain persons should be disobedient unto the words spoken by Him through us, let them understand that they will entangle themselves in no slight transgression and danger.

—St. Clement, *Letter to the Corinthians,* c. 95

✦

As the Son of God came to do the Father's will, so shall ye fulfill the will of your mother, which is the Church, the head of which, as has been stated already, is the church of Rome. Wherefore, whatsoever may be done against the discipline of this church, without the decision of justice, cannot on any account be permitted to be held valid.

—St. Callixtus, Letter to Bishop Benedict, c. 220

✦

Are you ignorant that the custom has been to write first to us and then for a just decision to be passed from this place [Rome]?

—St. Julius I, Letter on Behalf of Athanasius, 341

✦

The decrees I have carried out have never been my own but the apostles', that they might be forever confirmed and upheld.

—Liberius, Letter to Emperor Constantius, 355

✦

We are within that holy church in which the holy apostle [St. Peter] sat and taught us how we ought to guide the rudder which we have received.

—St. Damasus, Letter to the Eastern Bishops, 378

✦

The holy Roman Church has been placed at the forefront not by the conciliar decisions of other churches, but has received the primacy by the evangelic voice of our Lord and Savior.

—St. Damasus I, Decree of Damasus, 382

✦

The blessed apostle Peter . . . protects and watches over us, his heirs, as we trust, in all the care of his ministry.

—St. Siricius, Letter to Bishop Himerius of Tarragona, February 11, 385

✦

They did not regard anything as finished, even though it was the concern of distant and remote provinces, until it had come to the notice of this See [Rome], so that what was a just pronouncement might be confirmed by the authority of this See, and thence other churches—just as all waters proceed from their own natal source and, through the various regions of the whole world, remain pure liquids of an incorrupted head.

—St. Innocent I, Letter to the Council of Carthage, January 27, 417

✦

The tradition of the Fathers has attributed such great authority to the Apostolic See that no one would dare to disagree wholly with its judgment.

—St. Zosimus, Letter to the Bishops of Africa, March 21, 418

✦

It is clear that this Church [of Rome] is to all churches throughout the world as the head is to the members, and that whoever separates himself from it becomes an exile from the Christian religion.

—St. Boniface I, Letter to Rufus, Bishop of Thessaly, March 11, 422

✦

It has never been allowed that that be discussed again which has once been decided by the Apostolic See.

—St. Boniface I, Letter to Rufus, Bishop of Thessaly, March 11, 422

✦

Anyone who dares to secede from Peter's solid rock may understand that he has not part or lot in the divine mystery.

—St. Leo I, Letter to the Bishops of the Province of Vienne, July 1, 445

✦

If the hearts of the faithful should be submitted to all priests in general who rightly administer divine things, how much more should assent be given to the Bishop of that See which the Most High wished to be pre-eminent over all priests, and which the devotion of the whole Church has honored ever since.

—St. Gelasius I, Letter to the Emperor Anastasius, 494

✦

The Apostolic See's confession of faith is unassailable; it is impossible for it to be stained by any false doctrine or be contaminated by any error.

—St. Gelasius I, Letter to the Emperor Anastasius, 494

✦

It is clear to everyone who knows the Gospel that the care of the whole Church has been committed to the blessed Peter, chief of the apostles.

—St. Gregory I the Great, Letter to the Emperor Maurice, c. 595

✦

The Roman See has never erred, and never will err, because of Christ's promise.

—St. Agatho, Letter to the Synod at Constantinople, 680

✦

The pontiffs who have ruled at Rome preside there in order to maintain peace, like a wall joining East and West, occupying the middle ground between them . . . [the] arbitrators and promoters of peace.

—Gregory II, Letter to Emperor Leo II, 727

✦

The privileges of this See are perpetual: they were planted and rooted in by God Himself. They may be beaten against, but not changed; they may be attacked, but not destroyed.

—St. Nicholas I, Letter to Emperor Michael III, 863

✦

Neither fear nor favor nor any respect of persons shall, so far as in us lies, prevent us from claiming with God's help every possible honor due to Him whose servant we are.

—St. Gregory VII, Letter to Solomon, King of Hungary, October 1074

✦

While we, unworthy sinner that we are, stand in [Peter's] place of power, still whatever you send to us, whether in writing or by word of mouth, he himself receives, and while we read what is written or hear the voice of those who speak, he discerns with subtle insight from what spirit the message comes.

—Gregory VII, Letter to Emperor Henry IV, December 1075

✦

When God gave to Blessed Peter the princely power of binding and loosing in heaven and on earth, He made no exception, and withdrew nothing from his power.

—St. Gregory VII, Letter to Hermann, Bishop of Metz, March 1081

✦

No one, surely, of sound mind is ignorant that it belongs to our office to reprove any Christian for mortal sin, and if he disregards our punishment, to compel him by ecclesiastical censure.

—Innocent III, *Decretals*, c. 1207

✦

The Roman pontiffs, successors of Peter and vicars of Jesus Christ, succeeding each other in a remarkable line of succession through the ages, have received from the Lord the primacy and authority [magisterium] over all the churches and all the prelates of the Church, nay, over all the faithful.

—Innocent III, Letter to the King of the Armenians, c. 1207

✦

There is one body of this one and only Church, and one head.

—Boniface VIII, *Unam Sanctam*, November 18, 1302

✦

The Roman pontiff alone . . . has full jurisdiction and power to summon, to transfer, to dissolve councils, as is clear not only from the testimony of holy writ, from the teaching of the fathers and of the Roman pontiffs, and from the decrees of the sacred canons, but from the teaching of the very councils themselves.

—Leo X, *Pastor Aeternus,* December 19, 1516

✦

He who reigns on high, to Whom is given all power in Heaven and on earth, has entrusted His holy Catholic and Apostolic Church, outside which there is no salvation, to one person alone on earth, namely to Peter the Prince of the Apostles, and to Peter's successor, the Roman Pontiff.

—St. Pius V, *Regnans in Excelsis,* February 25, 1570

✦

The power of the Roman pontiff is supreme, universal, and absolutely independent, whereas the power of the bishops is fixed within definite limits and is not absolutely independent.

—Leo XIII, *Satis Cognitum,* 1896

✦

The history of all past ages is witness that the Apostolic See . . . has constantly adhered to the same doctrine, in the same sense and in the same mind.

—Leo XIII, *Testem Benevolentiae,* January 22, 1899

✦

Just what do these keys mean, which were entrusted personally to Simon son of John, to Peter, if they are not an indication of the universal rule over the Church which was entrusted to him?

—John XXIII, Address to the Lenten Preachers of Rome, February 22, 1962

XXII

THE CALL TO THE
RELIGIOUS LIFE

Behold, we have left all things and have followed thee.

—St. Peter, Mark 9:28, c. 30

✦

Now the Lord Jesus . . . desired that the Church, whose Bridegroom
he is, should have her visage shining with the splendor of chastity. . . .
Hence all we priests and Levites are bound by the unbreakable law of
those instructions to subdue our hearts and bodies to soberness and
modesty from the day of our ordination, that we may be wholly pleasing to our God in the sacrifices which we daily offer.

—St. Siricius, Letter to Himerius, Bishop of Tarragon,
February 10, 385

✦

No one does more harm to the Church than he, who having the
title or rank of holiness, acts evilly.

—St. Gregory I the Great, *Pastoral Care*, c. 590.

✦

I command you to apply yourself with more energy to preaching and enforcing the celibacy of the clergy according to the edicts of the Fathers.

—St. Gregory VII, Letter to Hanno, Archbishop of Cologne, March 29, 1075

✦

See that the bounds of common sense are not exceeded, however, for common sense is the guide of the virtues.

—Innocent IV, *Quae Honorem Conditoris Omnium,* October 1, 1247

✦

Far, far from the clergy be the love of novelty! God hateth the proud and the obstinate mind.

—St. Pius X, *Pascendi,* September 8, 1907

✦

Holy virginity and that perfect chastity which is consecrated to the service of God is without doubt among the most precious treasures which the Founder of the Church has left in heritage to the society which He established.

—Pius XII, *Sacra Virginitas*, March 25, 1954

✦

This then is the primary purpose, this the central idea of Christian virginity: to aim only at the divine, to turn thereto the whole mind and soul; to want to please God in everything, to think of Him continually, to consecrate body and soul completely to Him.

—Pius XII, *Sacra Virginitas,* March 25, 1954

✦

Priestly celibacy has been guarded by the Church for centuries as a brilliant jewel, and retains its value undiminished even in our time when the outlook of men and the state of the world have undergone such profound changes.

—Paul VI, *Sacerdotalis Caelibatus,* June 24, 1967

✦

Who can doubt the moral and spiritual richness of such a life, consecrated not to any human ideal, no matter how noble, but to Christ and to His work to bring about a new form of humanity in all places and for all generations?

—Paul VI, *Sacerdotalis Caelibatus,* June 24, 1967

✦

At times loneliness will weigh heavily on the priest, but he will not for that reason regret having generously chosen it. Christ, too, in the most tragic hours of His life was alone—abandoned by the very ones whom He had chosen as witnesses to, and companions of, His life, and whom He had loved "to the end"—but He stated, "I am not alone, for the Father is with me."

—Paul VI, *Sacerdotalis Caelibatus,* June 24, 1967

✦

Our world today stresses the positive values of love between the sexes but has also multiplied the difficulties and risks in this sphere. In order to safeguard his chastity with all care and affirm its sublime meaning, the priest must consider clearly and calmly his position as a man exposed to spiritual warfare against seductions of the flesh in himself and in the world, continually renewing his resolution to give an ever increasing and ever better perfection to the irrevocable offering of himself which obliges him to a fidelity that is complete, loyal and real.

—Paul VI, *Sacerdotalis Caelibatus,* June 24, 1967

✦

The Church, to a great extent, derives Her vigor, Her apostolic zeal, and Her fervor in seeking holiness of life, from the flourishing condition of Her Religious Institutes.

—Paul VI, Address to the General Chapters of Religious Orders and Congregations, May 23, 1964

✦

A vocation is a mystery of divine election.

—John Paul II, *Gift and Mystery,* 1996

XXIII

THE DUTY OF PASTORS

Lord, I am ready to go with thee both into prison and to death.

—St. Peter, Luke 22:33, c. 30

✦

Feed the flock of God which is among you, taking care of it, not by constraint, but willingly, according to God: not for filthy lucre's sake, but voluntarily. . . . And when the prince of pastors shall appear, you shall receive a never fading crown of glory.

—St. Peter, First Epistle 5:2,4, c. 45

✦

I understand that I am not at liberty to act otherwise than to expend all my efforts on that cause in which the well-being of the universal Church is at stake.

—St. Callixtus I, Letter to Bishop Benedict, c. 220

✦

Strive then as a good soldier, who expects reward from the everlasting Emperor.

—Liberius, Third Letter to Bishop Eusebius, 354

✦

Permit hereafter neither your clergy nor your laity to listen to vain reasonings and idle speculations.

—St. Damasus, Letter to the Eastern Bishops, 378

✦

No priest of the Lord is free to be ignorant of the statutes of the Apostolic See.

—St. Siricius, Letter to Bishop Himerius of Tarragona, February 11, 385

✦

It is felt right that a shepherd should bestow great care and watchfulness upon his flock. In like manner too from his lofty tower the careful watchman keeps a lookout day and night on behalf of the city. So also in the hour of tempest when the sea is dangerous the shipmaster suffers keen anxiety lest the gale and the violence of the waves shall dash his vessel upon the rocks.

—Anastasius I, Letter to Simplicianus, Bishop of Milan, 400

✦

It is with similar feelings that . . . our brother and fellow-bishop ceases not to watch over the things that make for salvation, that God's people in the different churches may not . . . run into awful blasphemies.

—Anastasius I, Letter to Simplicianus, Bishop of Milan, 400

✦

Nothing is more befitting the priestly office than the protection of the poor and the weak.

—St. Gelasius I, c. 494

✦

Two there are, august emperor, by which this world is chiefly ruled, the sacred authority of the priesthood and the royal power. Of these the responsibility of priests is more weighty in so far as they will answer for the kings of men themselves at the divine judgment.

—St. Gelasius I, Letter to the Emperor Anastasius, 494

✦

Let, then, neither the toil of the journey nor the tongues of evil-speaking men deter you; but with all constancy and all fervor go on with what under God's guidance you have commenced, knowing that great toil is followed by the glory of an eternal reward.

—St. Gregory I the Great, To the Benedictine Monks
Going to Evangelize England, 597

✦

Be zealously affected to command that in all the churches the pure tradition be held.

—St. Agatho I, Letter to the Third Council of Constantinople, November 15, 680

✦

From the tomb his call to the Church still rings out: "Watch lest the wolf rend God's flock."

—St. Sergius I, Inscription on the Tomb of Pope St. Leo I, 688

✦

We grieve to say it—we greatly fear that you will receive judgment, not as shepherds but as hirelings, who, seeing the wolf tearing the flock of the Lord, take to flight and hide yourselves in silence like dogs too weak to bark.

—St. Gregory VII to the Clergy of France, September 10, 1074

✦

Even though fear and peril of death should threaten you, still you ought not to surrender the independence of your priestly office.

—St. Gregory VII, Letter to the Clergy of France, September 10, 1074

✦

Since the days are evil and many things must be endured through the nature of the times, we beg you to be discreet, and we warn, advise and exhort you to show yourself wary, prudent and circumspect in all your actions for your own sake and that of the Church.

—Alexander III, Letter to St. Thomas Becket, Archbishop of Canterbury, 1165

✦

In churchmen indulgence is more fitting than severity.

—Alexander III, Letter to Louis VII of France, 1167

✦

Do not admit anyone to the clergy, entrust to no one the ministry of the mysteries of God, allow no one to hear confessions or preach sermons, do not transfer any administration or office to anyone, before you carefully weigh, examine and test their spirit to see if they are of God.

—Pius VII, *Diu Satis*, May 15, 1800

✦

Carefully investigate the directors given charge of boys and young men in seminaries and colleges, and the courses they are to follow, the teachers chosen for secondary schools, and the schools which are to be run. Keep out the ravening wolves who do not spare the flock of innocent lambs, and expel them if necessary by the way they entered.

—Pius VII, *Diu Satis*, May 15, 1800

✦

You must love above all things the beauty of God's house.

—Leo XII, *Caritate Christi,* December 25, 1825

✦

Guard the Church which I have loved so well and sacredly.

—Pius IX (dying words), 1878

✦

Venerable Brethren, of what nature and magnitude is the care that must be taken by you in forming the clergy to holiness! All other tasks must yield to this one.

—St. Pius X, *E Supremi,* October 4, 1903

✦

Wherefore the chief part of your diligence will be directed to governing and ordering your seminaries aright so that they may flourish equally in the soundness of their teaching and in the spotlessness of their morals.

—St. Pius X, *E Supremi*, October 4, 1903

✦

Remember that your duty is not the extension of a human realm, but of Christ's; and remember too that your goal is the acquisition of citizens for a heavenly fatherland, and not for an earthly one.

—Benedict XV, *Maximum Illud*, 1919

✦

For the preservation of the moral order . . . religious authority must enter in to enlighten the mind, to direct the will, and to strengthen human frailty by the aid of divine grace.

—Pius XI, *Casti Connubii*, December 31, 1930

✦

Never be discouraged by the difficulties that arise, and never let your pastoral zeal grow cold.

—Pius XII, *Mediator Dei*, November 20, 1947

✦

Let the priest not trust in his own strength nor be complacent in his own gifts nor seek the esteem and praise of men but let him imitate Christ, Who "did not come to be served but to serve."

—Pius XII, *Menti Nostrae*, September 23, 1950

✦

"Watch and pray," mindful that your hands touch those things which are most holy, that you have been consecrated to God and are to serve Him alone.

—Pius XII, *Menti Nostrae*, September 23, 1950

✦

Visit your parishioners in their homes. . . . It is a pastoral practice that should not be neglected. Teach your people boldly about the faithful love of God. And do not forget all those with special needs, particularly those who are in prison, and their families.

—John Paul II, *The Seven Sacraments*, October, 1982

✦

The Church's pastors, in communion with the Successor of Peter, are close to the faithful in this effort; they guide and accompany them by their authoritative teaching, finding ever new ways of speaking with love and mercy not only to believers but to all people of good will.

—John Paul II, *Veritatis Splendor,* August 6, 1993

＊

Make sure that in theological faculties, seminaries and Catholic institutions sound doctrine is taught, explained and more fully investigated.

—John Paul II, *Evangelium Vitae,* March 25, 1995

＊

Without the virtues of self-discipline, diligent contemplation of the truth, simplicity of life and joyful dedication to others, you will not have the inner strength to combat the culture of death which is threatening the modern world.

—John Paul II, Address at Sacred Heart Cathedral, Newark, New Jersey, October 4, 1995

＊

I urge you to pray each day: "O good Jesus, make me a priest like unto your own Heart."

—John Paul II, Address at Sacred Heart Cathedral, Newark, New Jersey, October 4, 1995

＊

What does it mean to be a priest? According to Saint Paul, it means above all to be a steward of the mysteries of God.

—John Paul II, *Gift and Mystery,* 1996

＊

The priest receives from Christ the treasures of salvation, in order duly to distribute them among the people to whom he is sent.

—John Paul II, *Gift and Mystery,* 1996

＊

In every situation, [the priest's] task is to show God to man as the final end of his personal existence. The priest becomes the one to whom people confide the things most dear to them and their secrets, which are sometimes very painful.

—John Paul II, Letter to Priests for Holy Thursday, March 17, 1996

✦

[The priest] becomes the one whom the sick, the elderly and the dying wait for, aware as they are that only he, a sharer in the priesthood of Christ, can help them in the final journey which is to lead them to God.

—John Paul II, Letter to Priests for Holy Thursday, March 17, 1996

✦

An intimate bond unites our priesthood to the Holy Spirit and to his mission.

—John Paul II, Letter to Priests for Holy Thursday, March 17, 1996

✦

On the day of our priestly ordination, by virtue of a unique outpouring of the Paraclete, the Risen One accomplished again in each of us what he accomplished in his disciples on the evening of Easter.

—John Paul II, Letter to Priests for Holy Thursday, March 17, 1996

XXIV

THE VOCATION OF THE LAITY

You are a chosen generation, a kingly priesthood, a holy nation, a purchased people: that you may declare his virtues who hath called you out of darkness into his marvelous light.

—St. Peter, First Epistle 1:9, c. 45

✦

Each of us, brethren, must in his own place please God with a good conscience.

—St. Clement I, *Letter to the Corinthians,* c. 95

✦

Every Christian king when he approaches his end asks the aid of a priest as a miserable suppliant that he may escape the prison of hell, may pass from darkness into light and may appear at the judgment seat of God freed from the bonds of sin. But who, layman or priest, in his last moments has ever asked the help of any earthly king for the safety of his soul?

—St. Gregory VII, Letter to Hermann, Bishop of Metz, March 15, 1081

✦

All, moreover, are bound to love the Church as their common mother, to obey her laws, promote her honor, defend her rights, and to endeavor to make her respected and loved.

—Leo XIII, *Immortale Dei,* November 1, 1885

✦

It is not priests alone, but all the faithful without exception, who must concern themselves with the interests of God and souls.

—St. Pius X, *E Supremi,* October 4, 1903

✦

All the faithful make up a single and very compact body with Christ for its Head, and the Christian community is in duty bound to participate in the liturgical rites according to their station.

—Pius XII, *Mediator Dei*, November 20, 1947

✦

With docile hearts, then, let all Christians hearken to the voice of their Common Father [the Pope], who would have them, each and every one, intimately united with him as they approach the altar of God, professing the same faith, obedient to the same law, sharing in the same Sacrifice with a single intention and one sole desire.

—Pius XII, *Mediator Dei,* November 20, 1947

✦

In Our paternal care as universal Pastor of souls, We earnestly beg Our sons, immersed though they be in the business of this world, not to allow their consciences to sleep; not to lose sight of the true hierarchy of values.

—John XXIII, *Mater et Magistra,* May 15, 1961

✦

Take the greatest care to be inside the sheepfold of Christ and to be among the fortunate number of His flock.

—Paul VI, *Voi Forse Sapete*, June 1, 1966

＋

If they live by [the Church's] life, her members are sanctified; if they move away from her, they fall into sins and disorders that prevent the radiation of her sanctity.

—Paul VI, *Credo of the People of God,* June 30, 1968

＋

By enduring the toil of work in union with Christ crucified for us, man in a way collaborates with the Son of God for the redemption of humanity. He shows himself a true disciple of Christ by carrying the cross in his turn every day in the activity that he is called upon to perform.

—John Paul II, *Laborem Exercens,* September 14, 1981

＋

The denial of God deprives the person of his foundation. . . . The atheism of which we are speaking is also closely connected with the rationalism of the Enlightenment, which views human and social reality in a mechanistic way.

—John Paul II, *Centisimus Annus,* May 1, 1991

＋

Thus there is a denial of the supreme insight concerning man's true greatness, his transcendence in respect to earthly realities, the contradiction in his heart between the desire for the fullness of what is good and his own inability to attain it and, above all, the need for salvation which results from this situation.

—John Paul II, *Centisimus Annus,* May 1, 1991

＋

Our restless hearts seek beyond our limits, challenging our capacity to think and love: to think and love the immeasurable, the infinite, the absolute and supreme form of Being.

—John Paul II, *Christ Alone Gives Life*, August 14, 1993

✦

Our inner eye looks upon the unlimited horizons of our hopes and aspirations. And in the midst of all life's contradictions, we seek the true meaning of life.

—John Paul II, *Christ Alone Gives Life,* August 14, 1993

✦

You know how easy it is to avoid the fundamental questions. But your presence here shows that you will not hide from reality and from responsibility!

—John Paul II, *Christ Alone Gives Life,* August 14, 1993

✦

Have the courage to believe the Good News about life which Jesus teaches in the Gospel.

—John Paul II, *Christ Alone Gives Life,* August 14, 1993

✦

Open your minds and hearts to the beauty of all that God has made and to his special, personal love for each one of you.

—John Paul II, *Christ Alone Gives Life,* August 14, 1993

✦

Why do so many acquiesce in attitudes and behavior which offend human dignity and disfigure the image of God in us?

—John Paul II, *Christ Alone Gives Life,* August 14, 1993

✦

The normal thing would be for conscience to point out the mortal danger to the individual and to humanity contained in the easy acceptance of evil and sin. Is it because conscience itself is losing the ability to distinguish good from evil?

—John Paul II, *Christ Alone Gives Life,* August 14, 1993

✦

Do not stifle your conscience! Conscience is the most secret core and sanctuary of a person, where we are alone with God.

—John Paul II, *Christ Alone Gives Life,* August 14, 1993

✦

In discovering God's greatness, man discovers the unique position he holds in the visible world: "You have made him little less than the angels, and crowned him with glory and honor. You have given him rule over the works of your hands, putting all things under his feet" (Psalm 8:6–7).

—John Paul II, *Christ Alone Gives Life,* August 14, 1993

✦

Good Shepherd, teach the young people gathered here, teach the young people of the world, the meaning of "laying down" their lives through vocation and mission.

—John Paul II, *Christ Alone Gives Life,* August 14, 1993

✦

You know how, before his public life, Jesus retired in prayer for forty days in the desert. You too try to bring a little silence into your lives, so as to be able to think, to reflect, to pray with greater fervor and make resolutions with greater decision.

—John Paul II, Solitude and Silence Nourish Spiritual Life, 1998

✦

It is difficult to create "zones of desert and silence" these days because you are continually being overcome by the complications of your work, the uproar of events, the attraction of the communications media, so much so that inner peace is compromised and the supreme thoughts which ought to characterize man's existence are hindered. It is difficult, but it is possible and important to succeed in it.

—John Paul II, Solitude and Silence Nourish Spiritual Life, 1998

HUMAN LIBERTY

The eternal law of God is the sole standard and rule of human liberty.

—Leo XIII, Libertas, June 20, 1888

✦

Liberty, then, as We have said, belongs only to those who have the gift of reason or intelligence. Considered as to its nature, it is the faculty of choosing means fitted for the end proposed, for he is master of his actions who can choose one thing out of many.

—Leo XIII, Libertas, June 20, 1888

✦

The Church cannot approve of that liberty which begets a contempt of the most sacred laws of God, and casts off the obedience due to lawful authority, for this is not liberty so much as license, and is most correctly styled by St. Augustine the "liberty of self-ruin," and by the Apostle St. Peter the "cloak of malice."

—Leo XIII, Immortale Dei, November 1, 1885

✦

Since man by his reason understands innumerable things, linking and combining the future with the present, and since he is master of his own actions therefore, under the eternal law, and under the power of God most wisely ruling all things, he rules himself by the foresight of his own counsel.

—Leo XIII, *Rerum Novarum,* May 15, 1891

✦

No one may with impunity outrage the dignity of man, which God Himself treats with great reverence, nor impede his course to that level of perfection which accords with eternal life in heaven.

—Leo XIII, *Rerum Novarum,* May 15, 1891

✦

Individual liberty, freed from all bonds and all laws, all objective and social values, is in reality only a death-dealing anarchy.

—Pius XII, Address to the World Federal Government Movement, April 6, 1951

✦

This too must be listed among the rights of a human being, to honor God according to the sincere dictates of his own conscience, and therefore the right to practice his religion privately and publicly.

—John XXIII, *Pacem in Terris,* April 11, 1963

✦

For every fundamental human right draws its indestructible moral force from the natural law, which in granting it imposes a corresponding obligation.

—John XXIII, *Pacem in Terris,* April 11, 1963

✦

Those, therefore, who claim their own rights, yet altogether forget or neglect to carry out their respective duties, are people who build with one hand and destroy with the other.

—John XXIII, *Pacem in Terris*, April 11, 1963

✦

Nowadays it is sometimes held, though wrongly, that freedom is an end in itself, that each human being is free when he makes use of freedom as he wishes.

—John Paul II, *Redemptor Hominis,* March 4, 1979

✦

In reality, freedom is a great gift only when we know how to use it consciously for everything that is our true good.

—John Paul II, *Redemptor Hominis,* March 4, 1979

✦

There is no true freedom where life is not welcomed and loved; and there is no fullness of life except in freedom.

—John Paul II, *Evangelium Vitae,* March 25, 1995

✦

When freedom is detached from objective truth it becomes impossible to establish personal rights on a firm rational basis; and the ground is laid for society to be at the mercy of the unrestrained will of individuals or the oppressive totalitarianism of public authority.

—John Paul II, *Evangelium Vitae,* March 25, 1995

✦

Freedom-as-autonomy, by its single-minded focus on the autonomous will of the individual as the sole organizing principle of public life, dissolves the bonds of obligation between men and women, parents and children, the strong and the weak, majorities and minorities. The result is the breakdown of civil society, and a public life in which the only actors of consequence are the autonomous individual and the State. This, as the twentieth century ought to have taught us, is a sure prescription for tyranny.

—John Paul II, Address to American Bishops in Rome, July 1, 1998

XXVI

THE DEFENSE OF HUMAN RIGHTS

Honor all men. Love the brotherhood. Fear God. Honor the king.

—St. Peter, First Epistle 2:17, c. 45

✦

By nature a man is made superior to beasts, but not to other men.

—St. Gregory I the Great, *Pastoral Care,* c. 590

✦

Act wisely and manfully; do all things in charity, so that the oppressed may find you cautious defenders and oppressors may learn that you are lovers of justice.

—St. Gregory VII, Letter to Hugo, Bishop of Die, and
Hugo, Abbot of Cluny, August 22, 1078

✦

In accordance with the teachings of the Gospel, the equality of men consists in this: that all, having inherited the same nature, are called to the same most high dignity of the sons of God, and that, as one and the same end is set before all, each one is to be judged by the same law and will receive punishment or reward according to his deserts.

—Leo XIII, *Quod Apostolici Muneris,* December 28, 1878

✦

To misuse men as though they were things in the pursuit of gain, or to value them solely for their physical powers—that is truly shameful and inhuman.

—Leo XIII, *Rerum Novarum,* May 15, 1891

✦

Every man has a right by nature to possess property as his own.

—Leo XIII, *Rerum Novarum,* May 15, 1891

✦

We must not be so insistent upon demanding our rights as in discharging our obligations.

—Benedict XV, Letter to the Bishop of Bergamo, 1920

✦

The Church teaches (she alone has been given by God the mandate and the right to teach with authority) that not only our acts as individuals but also as groups and as nations must conform to the eternal law of God.

—Pius XI, *Ubi Arcano Dei Consilio*, December 23, 1922

✦

To stifle the opinions of citizens, to reduce them forcibly to silence, is, in the eyes of every Christian, an outrage on the natural rights of man.

—Pius XII, Address to the International Convention of Catholic Press, February 18, 1950

✦

To send someone to a concentration camp and keep him there without any regular trial is a mockery of law.

> —Pius XII, Address to the 6th International Congress of Penal Law,
> October 3, 1953

✦

The right to existence, the right to respect from others and to one's good name, the right to one's own culture and national character, the right to develop oneself . . . are dictated by nature herself.

> —Pius XII, *The World Community,* December 6, 1953

✦

The Gospel of God's love for man, the Gospel of the dignity of the person and the Gospel of life are a single and indivisible Gospel.

> —John Paul II, *Evangelium Vitae,* March 25, 1995

✦

Human rights is based precisely on the affirmation that the human person, unlike animals and things, cannot be subjected to domination by others.

> —John Paul II, *Evangelium Vitae*, March 25, 1995

✦

The value of democracy stands or falls with the values which it embodies and promotes . . . values such as the dignity of every human person, respect for inviolable and inalienable rights, and the adoption of the "common good" as the end and criterion regulating political life.

> —John Paul II, *Evangelium Vitae,* March 25, 1995

✦

Where God is denied and people live as though he did not exist, or his commandments are not taken into account, the dignity of the human person and the inviolability of human life also end up being rejected or compromised.

—John Paul II, *Evangelium Vitae,* March 25, 1995

✦

Democracy serves what is true and right when it safeguards the dignity of every human person, when it respects inviolable and inalienable human rights, when it makes the common good the end and criterion regulating all public and social life. But these values themselves must have an objective content. Otherwise they correspond only to the power of the majority, or the wishes of the most vocal.

—John Paul II, Farewell Address to the People of the United States,
October 8, 1995

✦

It is now the dead of night. As we contemplate Christ dead on the Cross, our thoughts turn to the countless injustices and sufferings which prolong his passion in every part of the world.

—John Paul II, Address at the Stations of the Cross, April 10, 1998

✦

In every person suffering from hatred and violence, or rejected by selfishness and indifference, Christ continues to suffer and die. On the faces of those who have been "defeated by life" there appear the features of the face of Christ dying on the Cross.

—John Paul II, Address at the Stations of the Cross, April 10, 1998

✦

If there is no objective standard to help adjudicate between different conceptions of the personal and common good, then democratic politics is reduced to a raw contest for power.

—John Paul II, Address to American Bishops in Rome, July 1, 1998

✦

If constitutional and statutory law are not held accountable to the objective moral law, the first casualties are justice and equity, for they become matters of personal opinion.

—John Paul II, Address to American Bishops in Rome, July 1, 1998

✦

In dismantling barriers of race, social status and gender, Christianity proclaimed from the first the equality of all men and women before God.

—John Paul II, *Fides et Ratio,* September 14, 1998

XXVII

THE SANCTITY OF LIFE

God is the Author of all life, but his creation of human beings has a special character because God fashions them in his own image and creates them so they may come to know, love, and serve him in this life and be happy with him forever in the next. This unique relationship of God and humankind—no other creatures enjoy such a bond with their Creator—makes human life holy, and the taking of it a grave offense. We know that the deliberate killing of an innocent provokes God's wrath. "What hast thou done?" God asked Cain. "The voice of thy brother's blood crieth to me from the earth" (Genesis 4:10).

For these reasons, the Church has always taught that human life must be respected from the moment of conception. "You shall not abort a child or commit infanticide," says *The Didache,* the earliest surviving Christian catechetical text, dating from about A.D. 70.

Similarly, the Church finds euthanasia—intentionally using lethal injection or the cutting off of food and water to end the life of the sick, the handicapped, or the dying—morally objectionable.

In the mind of the Church, the right to life is granted by God to all of his human creatures. An American might say that this right is inalienable. It is not the concession of the state or of society, nor may it even be subject to the will of families.

The Church recognizes, however, certain situations in which a human life may be taken—to defend oneself or to defend another from an aggressor, for example. Throughout the centuries, the Church also has conceded society's right to defend itself by taking the life of violent criminals. At the same time, the popes have often appealed to secular authorities to spare the life of a male-factor, a tradition in which Pope John Paul II has been especially active.

✦ ✦ ✦

If he who destroys what is conceived in the womb by abortion is a murderer, how much more is he unable to excuse himself of murder who kills a child even one day old.

—Stephen V, Epistle to Archbishop of Mainz, September 14, 887

✦

To preserve one's life is a duty common to all individuals, and to neglect this duty is a crime.

—Leo XIII, *Rerum Novarum,* May 15, 1891

✦

The transmission of human life is the result of a personal and conscious act, and, as such, is subject to the all-holy, inviolable and immutable laws of God, which no man may ignore or disobey.

—John XXIII, *Mater et Magistra,* May 15, 1961

✦

Human life is sacred—all men must recognize that fact. From its very inception it reveals the creating hand of God. Those who violate His laws not only offend the divine majesty and degrade themselves and humanity, they also sap the vitality of the political community of which they are members.

—John XXII, *Mater et Magistra,* May 15, 1961

✦

Birth, like every other problem regarding human life, is to be considered, beyond partial perspectives—whether of the biological or psychological, demographic or sociological orders—in the light of an integral vision of man and of his vocation, not only his natural and earthly, but also his supernatural and eternal vocation.

—Paul VI, *Humanae Vitae,* July 25, 1968

✦

Our Christian conscience should be deeply concerned about the way in which sins against love and against life are often presented as examples of "progress" and emancipation. Most often, are they not but the age-old forms of selfishness dressed up in a new language and presented in a new cultural framework?

—John Paul II, Address at Williams-Brice Stadium, South Carolina, September 11, 1987

✦

It is very alarming to see governments in many countries launching systematic campaigns against birth, contrary not only to the cultural and religious identity of the countries themselves but also contrary to the nature of true development.

—John Paul II, *Sollicitudo Rei Socialis,* December 30, 1987

✦

It often happens that these campaigns [against life] are the result of pressure and financing coming from abroad, and in some cases they are made a condition for the granting of financial and economic aid and assistance. . . . Men and women [are] often subjected to intolerable pressures, including economic ones, in order to force them to submit to this new form of oppression.

—John Paul II, *Sollicitudo Rei Socialis,* December 30, 1987

✦

Human ingenuity seems to be directed more towards limiting, suppressing or destroying the sources of life—including recourse to abortion, which unfortunately is so widespread in the world—than towards defending and opening up the possibilities of life.

—John Paul II, *Centisimus Annus,* May 1, 1991

✦

However serious and disturbing the phenomenon of the widespread destruction of so many human lives, either in the womb or in old age, no less serious and disturbing is the blunting of the moral sensitivity of people's consciences.

—John Paul II, *On Combatting Abortion and Euthanasia,* May 19, 1991

✦

From Christ [the Church] receives the "Gospel of life" and . . . even at the price of going against the trend, she must proclaim that Gospel courageously and fearlessly, in word and deed, to individuals, peoples and states.

—John Paul II, *On Combatting Abortion and Euthanasia,* May 19, 1991

✦

Our theme is life, and life is full of mystery.

—John Paul II, *Christ Alone Gives Life,* August 14, 1993

✦

Science and technology have made great progress in discovering the secrets of our natural life; however, even a superficial look at our personal experience shows that there are many other dimen sions to individual and collective life on this planet.

—John Paul II, *Christ Alone Gives Life,* August 14, 1993

✦

With time the threats against life have not grown weaker. They are taking on vast proportions. They are not only threats coming from the outside, from the forces of nature or the "Cains" who kill the "Abels"; no, they are scientifically and systematically programmed threats.

—John Paul II, *Christ Alone Gives Life,* August 14, 1993

✦

The twentieth century will have been an era of massive attacks on life, an endless series of wars and a continual taking of innocent human life. False prophets and false teachers have had the greatest success.

—John Paul II, *Christ Alone Gives Life,* August 14, 1993

✦

We are also witnessing the spread of a mentality which militates against life—an attitude of hostility towards life in the mother's womb and life in its last phases.

—John Paul II, *Christ Alone Gives Life,* August 14, 1993

✦

At the very time that science and medicine are increasingly able to safeguard health and life, threats against life are becoming more insidious.

—John Paul II, *Christ Alone Gives Life,* August 14, 1993

✦

Abortion and euthanasia—the actual taking of a real human life— are claimed as "rights and solutions to problems," problems of individuals or those of society.

—John Paul II, *Christ Alone Gives Life,* August 14, 1993

✦

The killing of the innocent is no less sinful an act or less destructive because it is done in a legal and scientific manner.

—John Paul II, *Christ Alone Gives Life,* August 14, 1993

✦

In modern metropolises, life—God's first gift and a fundamental right of each individual, the basis of all other rights—is often treated more or less as a commodity to be controlled, marketed and manipulated at will.

—John Paul II, *Christ Alone Gives Life,* August 14, 1993

✦

Even in the midst of difficulties and uncertainties, every person sincerely open to truth and goodness can, by the light of reason and the hidden action of grace, come to recognize in the natural law written in the heart the sacred value of human life from its very beginning until its end.

—John Paul II, *Evangelium Vitae,* March 25, 1995

✦

Not only is the fact of the destruction of so many human lives still to be born or in their final stage extremely grave and disturbing, but no less grave and disturbing is the fact that conscience itself, darkened as it were by such widespread conditioning, is finding it increasingly difficult to distinguish between good and evil in what concerns the basic value of human life.

—John Paul II, *Evangelium Vitae,* March 25, 1995

✦

In the name of God: respect, protect, love, and serve life, every human life.

—John Paul II, *Evangelium Vitae,* March 25, 1995

◆

Life, especially human life, belongs only to God: for this reason whoever attacks human life, in some way attacks God himself.

—John Paul II, *Evangelium Vitae,* March 25, 1995

◆

The contemporary scene, moreover, is becoming even more alarming by reason of the proposals . . . to justify even infanticide, following the same arguments used to justify abortion. In this way, we revert to a state of barbarism which one hoped had been left behind forever.

—John Paul II, *Evangelium Vitae,* March 25, 1995

◆

By the authority which Christ conferred upon Peter and his Successors, and in communion with the Bishops of the Catholic Church, I confirm that the direct and voluntary killing of an innocent human being is always gravely immoral.

—John Paul II, *Evangelium Vitae,* March 25, 1995

◆

When the unborn child—the stranger in the womb—is declared to be beyond the protection of society, not only are America's deepest traditions radically undermined and endangered, but a moral blight is brought upon society.

—John Paul II, Homily at Giants Stadium, New Jersey, October 5, 1995

◆

When innocent human beings are declared inconvenient or burdensome, and thus unworthy of legal and social protection, grievous damage is done to the moral foundations of the democratic community.

—John Paul II, Homily at Giants Stadium, New Jersey, October 5, 1995

✦

The right to life is the first of all rights. It is the foundation of democratic liberties and the keystone of the edifice of civil society.

—John Paul II, Homily at Giants Stadium, New Jersey, October 5, 1995

✦

You are called to stand up for life! To respect and defend the mystery of life always and everywhere, including the lives of unborn babies, giving real help and encouragement to mothers in difficult situations.

—John Paul II, Homily in Central Park, New York City, October 7, 1995

✦

Stand up for the life of the aged and the handicapped, against attempts to promote assisted suicide and euthanasia! Stand up for marriage and family life! Stand up for purity!

—John Paul II, Homily in Central Park, New York City, October 7, 1995

✦

Resist the pressures and temptations of a world that too often tries to ignore a most fundamental truth: that every life is a gift from God our Creator, and that we must give an account to God of how we use it either for good or evil.

—John Paul II, Homily in Central Park, New York City, October 7, 1995

✦

Life, one's own and that of others, cannot be disposed of at will: it belongs to the Author of life.

—John Paul II, *Every Human Life Is Sacred,* February 2, 1997

✦

The historic and pressing moment has come to take a decisive step for civilization and the authentic welfare of peoples: the necessary step to reclaim the full human dignity and the right to life of every human being from the first instant of life and throughout the whole prenatal stage.

—John Paul II, Address to Members of the Pontifical Academy for Life,
February 14, 1997

✦

When the Church teaches, for example, that abortion, sterilization or euthanasia are always morally inadmissible, she is giving expression to the universal moral law inscribed on the human heart, and is therefore teaching something which is binding on everyone's conscience. Her absolute prohibition that such procedures be carried out in Catholic health-care facilities is simply an act of fidelity to God's law.

—John Paul II, Address to American Bishops in Rome, July 1, 1998

THE POPES AND SLAVERY

I t must be admitted that the Catholic Church's record on slavery is erratic. On the one hand, beginning in 1435, we have forceful condemnations of slavery by six popes. On the other hand, we find a mass of documents from popes, bishops, councils, and moral theologians speaking in support of slavery. It is not the record one would hope for. Those half-dozen Holy Fathers may have been voices crying in the wilderness, but it was their voices that were finally heard.

Although Christ never directly addressed the issue of slavery, his saying from the Sermon on the Mount, "All things therefore whatsoever you would that men should do to you, do you also to them" (Matthew 7:12), certainly could be applied to it and would in time lead to the abolition of slavery. By making no distinction between slaves and free-born when they preached the gospel, by recognizing that in the eyes of God all human beings were equal and worthy of salvation, the apostles, wittingly or unwittingly, were undermining an essential principle of slavery. The early Church's belief in the fundamental equality of all humankind was expressed most eloquently by St. Paul: "There is neither Jew nor Greek: there is neither bond nor free: there is neither male nor female. For you are all one in Christ Jesus" (Galatians 3:28).

It is important to bear in mind that two thousand years ago, slaves were as ubiquitous as employees are today. And they were just as essential to the economy. If it was beyond the apostles' power to destroy slavery, they were at least eager to mitigate it by providing a Christian framework in which masters and slaves would operate.

Once again, we turn to St. Paul: "Servants, obey in all things your masters according to the flesh . . . in simplicity of heart, fearing God. . . . Masters, do to your servants that which is just and equal: knowing that you also have a master in heaven" (Galatians 3:22, 4:1). Echoing St. Paul, St. Peter writes, "Servants, be subject to your masters with all fear, not only to the good and gentle, but also to the froward. For this is thankworthy, if for conscience toward God, a man endure sorrows, suffering wrongfully" (1 Peter 2:18–19).

A milestone in the Church's thinking about slavery emerged around 380, when St. Gregory of Nazianzen attempted to explain why slavery existed. St. Gregory said that in Eden, man had been created by God to be free. After the Fall, all manner of evil entered the world, including sickness, pain, death, and chattel slavery. St. Augustine, St. Basil, St. John Chrysostom, St. Thomas Aquinas, and St. Bonaventure are just a few of the Fathers who accepted St. Gregory's theory that slavery was inevitable, yet another manifestation of original sin.

There were, however, antislavery champions, most notably St. Gregory of Nyssa, who, about 385, preached the first antislavery sermon. In the late twelfth century, Blessed John Duns Scotus taught that slavery violates natural law and is acceptable under only two conditions: the person voluntarily gives himself or herself up to a life of perpetual servitude, or the person has been convicted of a crime and sentenced to penal labor by the state. Duns Scotus went on to argue that when St. Peter and St. Paul counseled slaves to obey their masters and masters to be just to their slaves, the apostles were trying to improve a bad situation. It was not Peter and

Paul's intention, according to Duns Scotus, to suggest that slavery was a legitimate institution.

By Duns Scotus's day, slavery in western Europe had almost disappeared. Two events in the fifteenth century revived the slave trade: the ongoing war between Christians and Muslims, and the exploration of Africa, Asia, and the Americas.

From the rise of Islam in the eighth century, Christians and Muslims had been at odds, and both sides enslaved prisoners captured in war. (Around the year 1218, St. Peter Nolasco and St. Raymond Peñafort founded the Mercedarians to ransom Christians held by the Moors.) By the fifteenth century, warfare between Christians and Muslims had escalated, and the sale of prisoners of war, especially to serve in the galleys, had grown with it. Suddenly there were slave markets in European cities that had not seen such a thing in centuries.

At the same time, the Portuguese were sending explorers along the coast of Africa to Asia in search of new trade routes. Almost everywhere they went, the Europeans discovered new opportunities to enrich themselves. They also found that their superior force of arms gave them the power to subdue and enslave the local people. This is what happened in the Canary Islands, one of the first "new lands" colonized by the Portuguese. On January 13, 1435, Pope Eugenius IV wrote Bishop Ferdinand on the island of Lanzarote denouncing the enslavement of the native population and demanding that the slaves be freed. He gave the Europeans in the Canary Islands fifteen days to liberate their slaves or incur the penalty of excommunication.

As the age of exploration continued, Pope Eugenius's teaching was forgotten. The saintly missionary bishop, Bartolomé de las Casas, tells how on the Fourth Sunday of Advent in 1511, at Concepción de la Vega on Hispaniola—an island today divided between

Haiti and the Dominican Republic—Father Antonio de Montesinos preached a fiery sermon denouncing the Spanish colonists for their barbarous cruelty to the Indians and assuring his audience that slavery was a mortal sin.

The next major statement from Rome came in 1537. Pope Paul III published a document attacking the notion that Indians could be enslaved because they were less than human. In spite of the Pope's assertion that "the Indians themselves indeed are true men," slave traders and slave owners would continue to argue that their slaves were subhuman, until slavery was finally abolished in the nineteenth century.

The pronouncements of Eugenius IV and Paul III notwithstanding, most of the popes of the fifteenth and sixteenth centuries—Nicholas V, Callixtus III, Sixtus IV, Alexander VI, Leo X—reaffirmed the right, founded in ancient Roman civil law, of monarchs to enslave captives taken in a just war. Conquistadors and colonists were delighted by this rationale and exploited it to make slaves of Native Americans, Africans, and Asians.

Around the year 1830, Johann Sailer, Bishop of Ratisbon in Germany, revived the spirit of St. Gregory of Nyssa and Paul III. "The state of slavery," Bishop Sailer said, "and any treatment of human beings as slaves, turns people who are persons into mere things, turns people who are ends in themselves into mere means, and does not allow the responsibility of people for what they do, or do not do, to develop properly, and in this way cripples them in their very humanity; hence it is contrary to the basic principles of all morality."

In 1839, Pope Gregory XVI revived the earlier papal antislavery teachings by publishing a document, *In Supremo*, that condemned the slave trade (and, by extension, slavery itself). The document caused some consternation in the United States, where the debate over slavery was becoming increasingly violent. In a series of open letters addressed to John Forsyth, President Martin van Buren's secretary of state, John England, Bishop of Charleston, assured his readers that he, along with the Catholic bishops of Baltimore, Bardstown, New Orleans, St. Louis, Mobile, and Nashville, regarded the condemnation found in the Pope's letter "as treating of the 'slave trade,' and not as touching 'domestic slavery' " as it existed in the United States.

The Civil War put an end to slavery in the United States. In other parts of the world, however, slavery lived on. When Brazil finally abolished slavery in its empire in 1888, Pope Leo XIII sent a celebratory letter to the bishops. Two years later he wrote to the bishops of the world urging them to raise their voices against "this gloomy plague of slavery" that survived in Africa.

The antislavery teaching of those handful of heroic popes found its final expression in *Gaudium et Spes*, the Constitution of the Church in the modern world promulgated by the Fathers of the Second Vatican Council on December 7, 1965. "Whatever is opposed to life itself," the Council Fathers wrote, "such as any type of murder, genocide, abortion, euthanasia or willful self-destruction; whatever violates the integrity of the human person, such as mutilation, torments inflicted on body or mind, attempts to coerce the will itself; whatever insults human dignity, such as subhuman living conditions, arbitrary imprisonment, deportation, slavery, prostitution, the selling of women and children; as well as disgraceful working conditions, where men are treated as mere tools for profit, rather than as free and responsible persons; all these things and others of their like are infamies indeed. They poison human society, but they do more harm to those who practice them than those who suffer from the injury. Moreover, they are a supreme dishonor to the Creator."

Firmly rooted in the teaching of Christ and his Apostles, guided by the witness of the saints, the Church has condemned slavery unequivocally. It has been a long, painful pilgrimage, but as Dr. Martin Luther King, Jr., said in 1964 when he accepted the Nobel Peace Prize, "Unarmed truth and unconditional love will have the final word in reality. This is why right temporarily defeated is stronger than evil triumphant."

✦ ✦ ✦

It is a salutary deed to restore by the benefaction of manumission to the state of liberty in which they were born, men whom nature originally begot free but whom the law of nations subjected to slavery.

—St. Gregory I the Great, Document Freeing the Slaves
Montana and Thomas, 595

✦

There is one thing about which we should give you a paternal admonition, and unless you emend, you incur a great sin . . . many in your area, being taken captive by pagans, are sold and are bought by your people and held under the yoke of slavery.

—John VIII, Letter to the Princes of Sardinia, 873

✦

It is evident that it is a religious duty and holy, as becomes Christians, that when your people have bought [slaves] from the Greeks themselves, for the love of Christ they set them free, and receive gain not from men, but from the Lord Jesus Christ Himself.

—John VIII, Letter to the Princes of Sardinia, 873

✦

Hence we exhort you and in fatherly love command that when you redeem some captives . . . for the salvation of your soul, you let them go free.

—John VIII, Letter to the Princes of Sardinia, 873

They have deprived the natives of their property or turned it to their own use, and have subjected some of the inhabitants of said islands to perpetual slavery, sold them to other persons and committed other various illicit and evil deeds against them.

—Eugenius IV, *Sicut Dudum*, January 13, 1435

✦

Therefore We . . . exhort, through the sprinkling of the Blood of Jesus Christ shed for their sins, one and all, temporal princes, lords, captains, armed men, barons, soldiers, nobles, communities and all others of every kind among the Christian faithful of whatever state, grade or condition, that they themselves desist from the aforementioned deeds, cause those subject to them to desist from them, and restrain them rigorously.

—Eugenius IV, *Sicut Dudum,* January 13, 1435

✦

And no less do We order and command all and each of the faithful of each sex that, within the space of fifteen days of the publication of these letters in the place where they live, they restore to their pristine liberty all and each person of either sex who were once residents of said Canary Islands . . . who have been made subject to slavery.

—Eugenius IV, *Sicut Dudum,* January 13, 1435

✦

These people are to be totally and perpetually free and are to be let go without the exaction or reception of any money.

—Eugenius IV, *Sicut Dudum,* January 13, 1435

✦

The Indians themselves, although they are outside the bosom of the Church . . . should not be deprived of their liberty . . . [and] they are not to be given into servitude.

—Paul III, *Pastorale Officium,* May 29, 1537

✦

No one in any way may presume to reduce said Indians to slavery.

—Paul III, *Pastorale Officium,* May 29, 1537

✦

Therefore, We, . . . noting that the Indians themselves indeed are true men and are not only capable of the Christian faith, but, as has been made known to us, promptly hasten to the faith, and wishing to provide suitable remedies for them, by our Apostolic Authority decree and declare by these present letters that the same Indians and all other peoples—even though they are outside the faith . . . should not be deprived of their liberty or of their possessions. . . . Rather they are to be able to use and enjoy this liberty and this ownership of property freely and licitly, and are not to be reduced to slavery, and that whatever happens to the contrary is to be considered null and void.

—Paul III, *Sublimis Deus,* June 2, 1537

✦

Under the penalty of excommunication . . . [if] anyone have or detain such Indian slaves they must give up all craft and deceit, set the slaves completely free and in the future neither make nor retain slaves in any way.

—Gregory XIV, *Cum Sicuti,* April 18, 1591

✦

[We] entrust to you the duty and command . . . that you severely prohibit anyone from reducing to slavery, selling, buying, exchanging, giving away, separating from wives and children, despoiling of their property, taking away to other places, depriving of liberty in any way and keeping in servitude said Indians.

—Urban VIII, *Commissum Nobis,* April 22, 1639

✦

The slave trade, although it has been somewhat diminished, is still carried on by numerous Christians. Therefore, desiring to remove such a great shame from all Christian peoples . . . and walking in the footsteps of Our Predecessors, We, by Apostolic authority, warn and strongly exhort in the Lord faithful Christians of every condition that no one in the future dare to bother unjustly, despoil of their possessions, or reduce to slavery Indians, Blacks or other such peoples.

—Gregory XVI, *In Supremo,* December 3, 1839

✦

[Christians are forbidden] to lend aid and favor to those who give themselves up to these practices, or exercise that inhuman traffic by which the Blacks, as if they were not humans but rather mere animals, having been brought into slavery in no matter what way, are, without any distinction and contrary to the rights of justice and humanity, bought, sold and sometimes given over to the hardest labor.

—Gregory XVI, *In Supremo,* December 3, 1839

✦

We prohibit and strictly forbid any Ecclesiastic or lay person from presuming to defend as permissible this trade in Blacks under no matter what pretext or excuse, or from publishing or teaching in any manner whatsoever, in public or privately, opinions contrary to what We have set forth in these Apostolic Letters.

—Gregory XVI, *In Supremo,* December 3, 1839

✦

The Supreme Author of all things so decreed that man should exercise a sort of royal dominion over beasts and cattle and fish and fowl, but never that men should exercise a like dominion over their fellow men.

—Leo XIII, *In Plurimis,* May 5, 1888

✦

Nothing is more base and wicked [than slavery].

—Leo XIII, *In Plurimis,* May 5, 1888

✦

Gorée . . . [is] the symbol of the appalling madness of those who reduced into slavery their brothers and sisters.

—John Paul II, Address at Gorée Island, February 22, 1992

✦

From this African shrine of black sorrow, we implore Heaven's forgiveness. . . . We pray that the scourge of slavery and all its effects may disappear forever.

—John Paul II, Address at Gorée Island, February 22, 1992

"You contradict God by perverting the natural law"

{*St. Gregory of Nyssa (c. 330–c. 395) was born in Caesarea, the capital of the Roman province of Cappadocia, which today is part of Turkey. It is no exaggeration to say that Gregory came from one of the greatest Christian families the Church has ever known. His mother Emmelia, his father Basil the Elder, and his paternal grandmother Macrina the Elder are honored as saints; his brothers included St. Basil the Great and St. Peter of Sebastea; St. Macrina the Younger was his sister. Although in his writings, Gregory is not so prolific as some of the other Doctors of the Church in the East, he certainly ranks among the most pro-*

*found. The following excerpts come from the fourth in a series of homilies St.
Gregory preached on the Book of Ecclesiastes.*}

✦

"I obtained servants and maidens" [Ecclesiastes 2:7]. What are you
saying? You condemn man who is free and autonomous to servitude, and you contradict God by perverting the natural law. Man,
who was created as lord over the earth, you have put under the
yoke of servitude as a transgressor and rebel against the divine precept. You have forgotten the limit of your authority which consists
in jurisdiction over brutish animals. Scripture says that man shall
rule birds, beasts, fish, four-footed animals and reptiles [Genesis
1.26]. How can you transgress against man's freedom. . . .

. . .

"I have obtained servants and maidens." What value is this, I ask?
What merit do you see in their nature? What small worth have you
bestowed upon them? What payment do you exchange for your
nature which God has fashioned? God has said, "Let us make man
according to our image and likeness" [Genesis 1:26]. Since we are
made according to God's likeness and are appointed to rule over
the entire earth, tell me, who is the person who sells and buys?

. . .

Oh, what a delusion! . . . suffering and cheerfulness, joy and sadness, grief and pleasure, wrath and fear, pain and death. Do not
these belong to both slave and lord who breathe the same air and
look upon the sun? Does not food nourish them both? Do not they
have the same intestines? Do not both become dust in death? Is
there not one standard? Is there not a common rule and a common
hell? How can you who are equal in all things have superiority so
that as man, you consider yourself as man's ruler and say "I have
servants and maidens" as if they were goats or cattle?

"Are these not men? Do they not have rational souls?"

{*On the Fourth Sunday of Advent, 1511, Father Antonio de Montesinos, a Dominican friar, preached a sensational sermon against the Spanish colonists who terrorized, enslaved, and even murdered the Indians of the New World. In the congregation that day was Admiral Diego Colon, son of Christopher Columbus. Neither he nor any of the colonists were moved by the sermon. Instead of freeing their slaves, the Spanish arranged to have Father Montesinos recalled to Spain.*}

✦ ✦ ✦

You are all in mortal sin, and live and die in it, because of the cruelty and tyranny you practice among these innocent peoples.

Tell me, by what right or justice do you hold these Indians in such a cruel and horrible servitude? On what authority have you waged such detestable wars against these peoples, who dwelt quietly and peacefully on their own land? Wars in which you have destroyed such infinite numbers of them by homicides and slaughters never before heard of? Why do you keep them so oppressed and exhausted, without giving them enough to eat or curing them of the sicknesses they incur from the excessive labor you give them, and they die, or rather, you kill them, in order to extract and acquire gold every day?

. . . Are these not men? Do they not have rational souls? Are you not bound to love them as you love yourselves? Don't you understand this? Don't you feel this? Why are you sleeping in such a profound lethargic slumber?

XXIX

THE POPES AND THE WORKERS

The Church has no commission from Christ to develop a specific social philosophy or an economic program. Nonetheless, at those points where the social order touches upon the moral order, the popes have always recognized their obligation to speak out.

Over the centuries, the popes have condemned usury, the slave trade, and the ritual murder libel against the Jews. Yet, in the nineteenth century, both industrialists and revolutionaries were certain that the Church had nothing to say about unbridled capitalism, or the rights of workers to a living wage and safe working conditions, or the legitimacy of labor unions and collective bargaining. So both capitalists and Marxists were shocked when Pope Leo XIII published his encyclical, *Rerum Novarum*, on May 15, 1891. In one eloquent document, Leo denounced "the inhumanity of employers . . . the unbridled greed of competitors," and defended the right of workers to form labor unions.

Leo XIII was not breaking new ground. In 1864 (the same year in which Karl Marx organized the First International), Wilhelm von Ketteler, Bishop of Mainz, published a book entitled *The Worker-Question and Christianity,* in which he argued that socialism was not entirely inconsistent with Catholicism. Cardinal

Henry Edward Manning, Archbishop of Westminster, had won international attention when he arbitrated the London dockworkers' strike of 1888. And in 1885, a French-Catholic industrialist named Lucien Harmel led one hundred of his workers on a pilgrimage to Rome, where they had an audience with Leo XIII. During the audience, Harmel and his employees described to the Pope their factory in Val-des-Bois, where Harmel offered his workers a comprehensive package of benefits, including health care, model housing, and a committee of workers and managers who made company policy. Furthermore, from the United States came word that Catholic workers were joining organizations such as the Knights of Labor, which did not appear to be Marxist or antireligious.

All of these factors played a part as Leo XIII crafted *Rerum Novarum.*

In *Rerum Novarum,* Leo XIII stated the Church's position plainly: it is intolerable that "a very few rich and exceedingly rich men have laid a yoke almost of slavery on the unnumbered masses of non-owning workers." He went on to say that Marxism's solution—war between the classes and the abolition of private property—is no solution at all: it violates the right to own property, which is guaranteed under natural law, and it thwarts enterprise. To the Marxists, Leo said that warfare can never resolve the inequalities that are an inevitable component of human life. To the owners, Leo said that what they owe to their workers is not charity, but justice.

At a time when owners and governments frequently employed troops to put down strikes, Leo XIII insisted that workers had legitimate grievances. Furthermore, he asserted that it was the state's obligation to pass legislation to eliminate the working conditions that prompted the workers to strike in the first place.

Succeeding popes built upon the social teaching of *Rerum Novarum*. John XXIII's *Mater et Magistra* expanded upon the principles Leo XIII had advocated. Pope John believed that workers should own a share of the companies they worked for, and he urged governments to take a more active role in overseeing the practices of the large corporations.

In *Populorum Progressio,* Pope Paul VI addressed the disparity of wealth among nations. He argued that the legacy of colonialism helped to keep the rich countries rich and the poor countries poor. He assailed free trade, saying that when there is an imbalance of power between two parties in a negotiation, the stronger of the two is most likely to enjoy the most generous terms. Furthermore, Pope Paul warned that if the imbalance was not corrected, the poor will be "sorely tempted to redress these insults to their human nature by violent means."

In *Sollicitudo Rei Socialis,* Pope John Paul II maintained that rivalry between the blocs of East and West (the encyclical was written before the collapse of the Soviet Empire) was one factor that impeded the economic development of the third world.

It may seem strange to say it, but there is one drawback to John Paul II's encyclical. From Leo XIII through Paul VI, the popes had built their arguments on natural law, which is comprised of principles of fairness and morality that all humankind can recognize by deductive reasoning. St. Thomas Aquinas was the most articulate promoter of natural law, and his theological method has guided Church teaching for seven hundred years. In *Sollicitudo Rei Socialis*, Pope John Paul II broke away from the Thomistic natural-law approach and rooted his encyclical almost exclusively in biblical texts. By appealing to natural law, Leo XIII and his successors could address their social teaching to all people of good will. By using the Bible as his primary point of reference, John Paul II may have inadvertently given the impression that in his encyclical he is speaking only to Christians.

The Church's social teaching is based upon a fundamental principle: all men and women are created in the image of God. As such, they enjoy certain rights and are subject to certain obligations. Critics of the Church's "intrusion" into the social, political, or economic sphere always insist that the Church's proper role is to remind its members of their religious duties. But these critics are in error. Christ established the Church not only to save souls, but also to heal human society.

LEO XIII, *RERUM NOVARUM,* MAY 15, 1891

The present age handed over the workers, each alone and defenseless, to the inhumanity of employers and the unbridled greed of competitors.

...

The whole process of production as well as trade in every kind of goods has been brought almost entirely under the power of a few, so that a very few rich and exceedingly rich men have laid a yoke almost of slavery on the unnumbered masses of non-owning workers.

...

When the worker places his energy and his labor at the disposal of another, he does so for the purpose of getting the means necessary for livelihood. He seeks in return for the work done, accordingly, a true and full right not only to demand his wage but to dispose of it as he sees fit.

...

Inasmuch as the Socialists seek to transfer the goods of private persons to the community at large, they make the lot of all wage earners worse, because in abolishing the freedom to dispose of wages, they take away from them by this very act the hope and the opportunity of increasing their property and of securing advantages for themselves.

...

Nature confers on man the right to possess things privately as his own.

...

The following [duties] concern the poor and the workers: To perform entirely and conscientiously whatever work has been voluntarily and equitably agreed upon; not in any way to injure the property or to harm the person of employers; in protecting their own interests, to refrain from violence and never to engage in rioting; not to associate with vicious men who craftily hold out exaggerated hopes and make huge promises, a course usually ending in vain regrets and in the destruction of wealth.

...

The following duties, on the other hand, concern rich men and employers: Workers are not to be treated as slaves; justice demands that the dignity of human personality be respected in them, ennobled as it has been through what we call the Christian character.

...

It is shameful and inhuman, however, to use men as things for gain and to put no more value on them than what they are worth in muscle and energy.

...

The threats pronounced by Jesus Christ, so unusual coming from Him, ought to cause the rich to fear; and that on one day the strictest account for the use of wealth must be rendered to God as Judge.

...

The favor of God Himself seems to incline more toward the unfortunate as a class; for Jesus Christ calls the poor blessed, and He invites most lovingly all who are in labor or sorrow to come to Him for solace, embracing with special love the lowly and those harassed by injustice.

...

If human society is to be healed, only a return to Christian life and institutions will heal it.

...

Equity therefore commands that public authority show proper concern for the worker so that from what he contributes to the common good he may receive what will enable him, housed, clothed, and secure, to live his life without hardship.

...

It is gratifying that societies of this kind [labor unions], composed either of workers alone or of workers and employers together, are being formed everywhere, and it is truly to be desired that they grow in number and in active vigor.

PIUS XI, *QUADRAGESIMO ANNO*, MAY 15, 1931

It is, nevertheless, an error to say that the economic and moral orders are so distinct from and alien to each other that the former depends in no way on the latter.

...

When the State brings private ownership into harmony with the needs of the common good, it does not commit a hostile act against private owners but rather does them a friendly service; for it thereby effectively prevents the private possession of goods, which the Author of nature in His most wise providence ordained for the support of human life, from causing intolerable evils and thus rushing to its own destruction; it does not destroy private possessions, but safeguards them; and it does not weaken private property rights, but strengthens them.

...

Property, that is, "capital," has undoubtedly long been able to appropriate too much to itself.

...

This concentration of power and might, the characteristic mark, as it were, of contemporary economic life, is the fruit that the unlimited freedom of struggle among competitors has of its own nature produced, and which lets only the strongest survive; and this is often the same as saying those who fight the most violently give least heed to their conscience.

...

If the class struggle abstains from enmities and mutual hatred, it gradually changes into an honest discussion of differences founded on a desire for justice, and if this is not that blessed social peace which we all seek, it can and ought to be the point of departure from which to move forward to the mutual cooperation of the industries and professions.

JOHN XXIII, *MATER ET MAGISTRA*, MAY 15, 1961

In the majority of cases a man's work is his sole means of livelihood. Its remuneration, therefore, cannot be made to depend on the state of the market. It must be determined by the laws of justice and equity.

...

We are filled with an overwhelming sadness when We contemplate the sorry spectacle of millions of workers in many lands and entire continents condemned through the inadequacy of their wages to live with their families in utterly sub-human conditions . . . [while] in some of these lands the enormous wealth, the unbridled luxury of the privileged few, stands in violent, offensive contrast to the utter poverty of the vast majority.

. . .

We therefore consider it Our duty to reaffirm that the remuneration of work is not something that can be left to the laws of the marketplace; nor should it be a decision left to the will of the more powerful. It must be determined in accordance with justice and equity; which means that workers must be paid a wage which allows them to live a truly human life and to fulfill their family obligations in a worthy manner.

. . .

The right of private ownership of goods, including productive goods, has permanent validity. It is part of the natural order.

. . .

The individual is prior to society and society must be ordered to the good of the individual.

. . .

The right of private ownership is clearly sanctioned by the Gospel.

. . .

The divine Master frequently extends to the rich the insistent invitation to convert their material goods into spiritual ones by conferring them on the poor. "Lay not up to yourselves treasures on earth; where the rust and moth consume and where thieves break through and steal. But lay up to yourselves treasures in heaven; where neither the rust nor moth doth consume, and where thieves do not break through nor steal" (Matthew 6:19–20).

. . .

It is nothing less than an outrage to justice and humanity to destroy or to squander goods that other people need for their very lives.

. . .

There is also a further temptation which the economically developed nations must resist: that of giving technical and financial aid with a view to gaining control over the political situation in the poorer countries, and furthering their own plans for world domination.

...

Let us be quite clear on this point. A nation that acted from these motives would in fact be introducing a new form of colonialism—cleverly disguised, no doubt, but actually reflecting that older, outdated type from which many nations have recently emerged. Such action would . . . constitute a menace to world peace.

...

Let men make all the technical and economic progress they can; there will be no peace nor justice in the world until they return to a sense of their dignity as creatures and sons of God, who is the first and final cause of all created being.

JOHN XXIII, *PACEM IN TERRIS,* APRIL 11, 1963

The Creator of the world has imprinted in man's heart an order which his conscience reveals to him and enjoins him to obey.

...

Beginning our discussion of the rights of man, we see that every man has the right to life, to bodily integrity, and to the means which are suitable for the proper development of life; these are primarily food, clothing, shelter, rest, medical care, and finally the necessary social services.

...

A human being also has the right to security in cases of sickness, inability to work, widowhood, old age, unemployment, or in any other case in which he is deprived of the means of subsistence through no fault of his own.

...

Human beings have the right to choose freely the state of life which they prefer, and therefore the right to set up a family, with equal rights and duties for man and woman, and also the right to follow a vocation to the priesthood or the religious life.

...

The right of every man to life is correlative with the duty to preserve it; his right to a decent standard of living with the duty of living it becomingly; and his right to investigate the truth freely, with the duty of seeking it ever more completely and profoundly.

...

It is not enough, for example, to acknowledge and respect every man's right to the means of subsistence if we do not strive to the best of our ability for a sufficient supply of what is necessary for his sustenance.

...

Inasmuch as God is the first Truth and the highest Good, He alone is that deepest source from which human society can draw its vitality, if that society is to be well ordered, beneficial, and in keeping with human dignity.

...

First among the rules governing the relations between States is that of truth. This calls, above all, for the elimination of every trace of racism.

PAUL VI, *POPULORUM PROGRESSIO*, MARCH 26, 1967

To seek to do more, know more and have more in order to be more: that is what men aspire to now when a greater number of them are condemned to live in conditions that make this lawful desire illusory.

...

In this confusion the temptation becomes stronger to risk being swept away towards types of messianism which give promises but create illusions. The resulting dangers are patent: violent popular reactions, agitation towards insurrection, and a drifting towards totalitarian ideologies.

···

Civilizations are born, develop and die. But humanity is advancing along the path of history like the waves of a rising tide encroaching gradually on the shore. We have inherited from past generations, and we have benefited from the work of our contemporaries: for this reason we have obligations towards all, and we cannot refuse to interest ourselves in those who will come after us to enlarge the human family.

···

All growth is ambivalent. It is essential if man is to develop as a man, but in a way it imprisons man if he considers it the supreme good.

···

If certain landed estates impede the general prosperity because they are extensive, unused or poorly used, or because they bring hardship to peoples or are detrimental to the interests of the country, the common good sometimes demands their expropriation.

···

A man by his work gives his imprint to it, acquiring, as he does so, perseverance, skill and a spirit of invention. Further, when work is done in common, when hope, hardship, ambition and joy are shared, it brings together and firmly unites the wills, minds and hearts of men: in its accomplishment, men find themselves to be brothers.

···

Work of course can have contrary effects, for it promises money, pleasure and power, invites some to selfishness, others to revolt.

···

We must make haste: too many are suffering, and the distance is growing that separates the progress of some and the stagnation, not to say the regression, of others.

···

The world is sick. Its illness consists less in the unproductive monopolization of resources by a small number of men than in the lack of brotherhood among individuals and peoples.

JOHN PAUL II, *SOLLICITUDO REI SOCIALIS,* DECEMBER 30, 1987

When the West gives the impression of abandoning itself to forms of growing and selfish isolation, and the East in its turn seems to ignore for questionable reasons its duty to cooperate in the task of alleviating human misery, then we are up against not only a betrayal of humanity's legitimate expectations—a betrayal that is a harbinger of unforeseeable consequences—but also of a real desertion of a moral obligation.

. . .

All of us experience firsthand the sad effects of this blind submission to pure consumerism: in the first place a crass materialism, and at the same time a radical dissatisfaction, because one quickly learns unless one is shielded from the flood of publicity and the ceaseless and tempting offers of products that the more one possesses the more one wants, while deeper aspirations remain unsatisfied and perhaps even stifled.

. . .

By virtue of her own evangelical duty, the Church feels called to take her stand beside the poor, to discern the justice of their requests, and to help satisfy them, without losing sight of the good of groups in the context of the common good.

. . .

The Church is an "expert in humanity," and this leads her necessarily to extend her religious mission to the various fields in which men and women expend their efforts in search of the always relative happiness which is possible in this world, in line with their dignity as persons.

...

Justice will never be fully attained unless people see in the poor person, who is asking for help in order to survive, not an annoyance or a burden, but an opportunity for showing kindness and a chance for greater enrichment.

XXX

THE POPES, THE NAZIS, AND THE HOLOCAUST

On October 12, 1997, an editorial in *The New York Times* asserted that Pope Pius XII "kept silent when he was given credible reports of the genocide and, after the war, helped Nazi war criminals escape justice." The *Times'* editorial was only the repetition of a slur first heard in February 1963 when Rolf Hochhuth's play, *The Deputy ("Der Stellvertreter")* debuted in Berlin. Hochhuth depicted Pius XII as a coldhearted bureaucrat, more concerned about the war's impact on Vatican finances than with the plight of the Jews.

Since 1963, Pius XII's detractors have expanded the charge, saying the Pope did not take any action to save the Jews because he was himself anti-Semitic.

Fifty-eight years ago, the notion that Pius was pro-Nazi would have been incomprehensible to the Nazis, the Italian Fascists, and their collaborators throughout Europe. They knew that Pius XII was one of their most determined opponents. And the accusation of criminal indifference to the plight of the victims of genocide would have stunned the tens of thousands (Israeli diplomat, Pinchas Lapide, says *hundreds* of thousands) of Jews whose lives were saved by the direct, personal intervention of the Pope.

"Why didn't the Pope say something?" is the great cry of the

> ## "In the long run, the Pope in Rome is a greater enemy."
>
> {*Contrary to conventional wisdom, the Nazis and the Italian Fascists knew that Popes Pius XI and Pius XII were their enemies. The excerpts that follow prove the point.*}
>
> ✦
>
> I do not underestimate [Pius XI's] strength, but he must not underestimate mine either. . . . A sign from me would be enough to unleash all the anti-clericalism of the Italian people who already find it hard enough to swallow a Jewish God.
>
> —Benito Mussolini to his foreign minister, Count Ciano, August 8, 1938
>
> The Church's obstruction of the practical solution of the Jewish problem constitutes a crime against the New Europe.
>
> —Roberto Farinacci, editor of Italy's official Fascist newspaper, *Regime Fascista,* October 1942

uninformed. In fact, Pius XII and his predecessor Pius XI said quite a lot—in public addresses, in private conversations, in official correspondence—to condemn the murderous policies of the Nazis against the Jews and the other victims of Fascism. The record of the Pope's words and actions during the war—*The Acts and Documents of the Holy See Relative to World War II*—fills ten volumes. But the Papacy's battle with the Third Reich predates the outbreak of the war.

In 1937, Pope Pius XI attacked National Socialism in an encyclic entitled *Mit brennender Sorge (With Deep Anxiety)*, which he addressed to the Catholic bishops of Germany. Although the encycli-

It is incomprehensible to the government that ecclesiastical circles, and especially the Catholic clergy, should today adduce so many protests against the elimination of the Jews.

—Prime Minister Vojtech Tuka of Slovakia, March 3, 1943

I'll go into the Vatican when I like. Do you think the Vatican worries me? We'll grab it. Yes, the whole diplomatic bunch is in there. I couldn't care less. That bunch in there, we'll drag them out, the whole swinish pack of them. What does it matter? We can apologize afterwards, that's nothing to worry about.

—Adolf Hitler, September 9, 1943

We should not forget that in the long run the Pope in Rome is a greater enemy of National Socialism than Churchill or Roosevelt.

—Reinhard Heydrich to his subordinates, May/June 1943

cal bore Pius XI's signature, Cardinal Eugenio Pacelli (later Pius XII) advised the Pope throughout the project and wrote large portions of the document himself. The Pope denounced the pagan cult Hitler was attempting to set up in his "German National Church," and he attacked the racism that was fundamental to National Socialism.

The Nazis never forgave Pius XI and Cardinal Pacelli for *Mit brennender sorge.* When Pius XI died in March 1939, the Nazi organ, *Das Reich,* smeared the Pope and the cardinal with the term they considered most vile. "Pius XI was a half-Jew, for his mother was a Dutch Jewess; but Cardinal Pacelli is a full Jew."

In fact, the Nazis had every reason to hate the new Pope, Pius XII. Within a few of weeks of the Nazi conquest of Poland, he was conspiring with the German opposition to overthrow Hitler, make peace with Great Britain, and end the war.

At the same time, Pius XII was working to frustrate the Nazis' anti-Semitic policies. In the autumn of 1940, the Pope won the release of about five hundred Jewish refugees who had been captured by Italian Fascists and were about to be handed over to the Germans. Pius XII built a settlement camp for the refugees in southern Calabria, where he fed, clothed, and protected them throughout the war. The men of the British 8th Army discovered the camp on December 23, 1943, and from the inmates themselves heard the story of how they had been saved by the Pope. A few days later, the 8th Army was greeted at Ferramonti–Tarsia near Cosenza by thirty-two hundred Jews, the entire population of another settlement camp under Vatican protection.

Word of the Holy See's work to rescue European Jews found its way to the United States. On January 2, 1940, the Chicago-based United Jewish Appeal for Refugees and Overseas Needs sent the Pope a contribution of $125,000 toward the Vatican's efforts to save "all those persecuted because of religion or race."

The Pope's efforts to save as many Jews as possible reached across Europe. Urged on by the Pope Monsignor Burzio, Papal Nuncio to Slovakia, launched an ambitious effort that hid some twenty-five thousand Slovak Jews in churches, monasteries, convents, and the homes of private individuals.

When Adolf Eichmann sent twenty-two thousand Hungarian Jews on the infamous "Death March," the Papal Nuncio in Budapest, Monsignor Angelo Rotta, immediately organized a relief convoy of food and medicine and ordered it to go after the exhausted, undernourished Jews. He also distributed Vatican safe-conducts among the marchers. Then he gave Sandor Gyorgy of the International Red Cross a letter stating that Gyorgy was "charged by the Apostolic Nunciature to locate on the roads and in camps persons of Jewish origin

"The people of Israel will never forget"

{As one European nation after another was liberated from the Nazis, expressions of thanks from chief rabbis, Jewish organizations, and individual Jews whose lives had been saved by the intervention of the Holy See and its representatives poured into Rome}.

✦

In the most difficult hours which we Jews of Romania have passed through, the generous assistance of the Holy See . . . was decisive and salutary. It is not easy for us to find the right words to express the warmth and consolation we experienced because of the concern of the supreme Pontiff, who offered a large sum to relieve the sufferings of deported Jews, sufferings which had been pointed out to him by you after your visit to Transnistria. The Jews of Romania will never forget these facts of historic importance.

> —Chief Rabbi Alexander Saffran of Bucharest, Romania, to Monsignor Andrea Cassulo, Papal Nuncio to Romania, April 7, 1944.

While our brothers were hunted, imprisoned and threatened with death in almost every country in Europe because they belonged to the Jewish people, Your Holiness has not only sent us large and generous gifts . . . but also has shown your lively fatherly interest in our physical, spiritual and moral well-being. In doing so, Your Holiness has as the first and highest authority upon earth fearlessly raised his universally respected voice, in the face of our powerful enemies, in order to defend openly our rights to the dignity of man.

continued

... When we were threatened with deportation to Poland, in 1942, Your Holiness extended his fatherly hand to protect us, and stopped the transfer of the Jews interned in Italy, thereby saving us from almost certain death.

—Jan Hermann and Dr. Max Pereles, the camp elders of Ferramonti–Tarsia, October 29, 1944

The people of Israel will never forget what His Holiness and his illustrious delegates, inspired by the eternal principles of religion which form the very foundations of true civilization, are doing for our unfortunate brothers and sisters in the most tragic hour of our history, which is living proof of divine Providence in this world.

—Chief Rabbi Isaac Herzog of Palestine, February 28, 1945

Allow us to ask the great honor of being able to thank personally His Holiness for the generosity he has shown us when we were persecuted during the terrible period of Nazi Fascism.

—Petition of twenty-thousand Jewish refugees from Central Europe to Pius XII, Summer 1945

When fearful martyrdom came to our people in the decade of Nazi terror, the voice of the Pope was raised for the victims. The life of our times was enriched by a voice speaking out on the great moral truths.

—Golda Meir in a cable to the Vatican expressing condolences at the death of Pius XII, 1958

who enjoy its diplomatic protection and to collect these." Thanks to Rotta and Gyorgy's efforts, some two thousand Jews were saved.

In the winter of 1944–45, the final months of the Nazi occupation of Budapest, Monsignor Rotta found himself in a half-bombed-out residence, his life in constant danger, and communications with the Vatican extremely difficult. He cabled Pope Pius to ask what he should do. The Pope answered, "If it is still possible to do some charity, remain!"

While there were limits to what Pius XII might accomplish in far-off places, he enjoyed more control in Italy, and in Rome particularly. In anticipation of the Nazis, he sent out by hand a letter to the bishops of Italy urging them "to save human lives by all means." He lifted the rule of enclosure so that cloistered convents and monasteries could hide Jews within sacred precincts where even the families of the monks and nuns could not set foot.

Inspired by the Pope, the Church in Italy—both religious and laity—responded with overwhelming courage. The Cardinal of Genoa hid at least eight hundred Jews. The Bishop of Assisi hid three hundred Jews for over two years, and even set up a synagogue in the monastery of St. Francis, where the refugees worshiped. The Bishop of Campagna, Giuseppe Maria Palatucci, worked with two members of his family, Father Alfonso Palatucci, Provincial of the Franciscans in Puglie, and Dr. Giovanni Palatucci, to save 961 Jews in Fiume. (Tragically, Dr. Palatucci's efforts were discovered and he was deported to Dachau, where he was killed.)

On October 16, 1943, the Nazi roundup of Rome's Jews began in earnest. There were an estimated ninety-five hundred Jews in the city at the time. Three Nazi police squads fanned out through Rome, yet only 1,259 people were taken. The overwhelming majority of Jews were already hiding—in the Vatican itself and in 155 Roman monasteries, convents, and churches.

The rescue effort was extraordinary. Consider, for example, the Pope's Palatine Guard. In 1942, it numbered three hundred men. By December 1943, there were four thousand names on the rolls, all of them carrying the invaluable papal passport. At least four hundred of these "guards" were Jews, of whom approximately 240 were sheltered inside Vatican City. An estimated three thousand Jews lived outside the city at the papal summer residence, Castel Gandolfo. In all, some forty thousand Jews throughout Italy were saved from the Nazis.

The heroism of Pope Pius XII and of Italy's Catholics during the war is nothing less than extraordinary. But there is another remarkable episode that is frequently overlooked. On February 13, 1945, in Rome's Basilica of Santa Maria degli Angeli, Israel Zolli, Chief Rabbi of Rome, and his wife Emma Majonica, were baptized into the Roman Catholic Church. At the font, Zolli took the name "Eugenio"—the Christian name of Pius XII.

Clearly, the charge that Pius XII was indifferent to the fate of the Jews is pure fantasy. The historical record proves that the Pope was not only active but heroic in his effort to save Jewish lives. Still, some detractors will always insist that Pius XII should have damned Hitler and excommunicated the Nazis. It is absurd to believe that a bull of excommunication would have stopped, even for a moment, men who were busily committing genocide.

Pius XII was not silent; he weighed his words. When the moment was opportune, he spoke his mind. But more to the point, he acted. And by his actions, many thousands of Jewish lives were saved.

✦ ✦ ✦

If it is a matter of saving a few souls, of averting even greater damage, we have the courage to negotiate even with the devil.

—Pius XI regarding the Vatican Concordat with the Third Reich, May, 1933

✦

[The Nazis] are in reality only miserable plagiarists who dress up old errors with new tinsel. It does not make any difference whether they flock to the banners of the social revolution, whether they are guided by a false conception of the world and of life, or whether they are possessed by the superstition of a race and blood cult.

—Eugenio Cardinal Pacelli to 250,000 Pilgrims at Lourdes, April 28, 1935

PIUS XI, MIT BRENNENDER SORGE, JULY 28, 1938

Whoever exalts race, or the people, or the State, or a particular form of State, or the depositories of power, or any other fundamental value of the worldly community . . . whoever raises these notions above their standard value and divinizes them to an idolatrous level, distorts and perverts an order of the world planned and created by God.

. . .

Whoever follows this so-called pre-Christian Germanic conception of substituting a dark and impersonal destiny for the personal God, denies thereby the Wisdom and Providence of God.

. . .

None but superficial minds could stumble into concepts of a national God, of a national religion; or attempt to lock within the frontiers of a single people, within the narrow limits of a single race, God, the Creator of the universe, King and Legislator of all nations, before whose immensity they are "as a drop in a bucket" [Isaiah 11:15].

. . .

The peak of the revelation as reached in the Gospel of Christ is final and permanent. It knows no retouches by human hand; it admits no substitutes or arbitrary alternatives such as certain leaders pretend to draw from the so-called myth of race and blood.

. . .

Should any man dare, in sacrilegious disregard of the essential differences between God and His creature, between the God-man and the children of man, to place a mortal, were he the greatest of all times, by the side of, or over, or against, Christ, he would deserve to be called prophet of nothingness.

...

The fool who has said in his heart, "There is no God" (Psalm 13:1), goes straight to moral corruption, and the number of these fools who today are out to sever morality from religion is legion.

...

We thank you, venerable Brethren, your priests and Faithful, who have persisted in their Christian duty and in the defense of God's rights in the teeth of an aggressive paganism.

...

The human race, the entire human race, is but a single and universal race of men. There is no room for special races. We may therefore ask ourselves why Italy should have felt a disgraceful need to imitate Germany.

✦

Mark well, we call Abraham our Patriarch, our ancestor. Anti-Semitism is irreconcilable with this lofty thought . . . Anti-Semitism is inadmissible; spiritually, we are all Semites.

—Pius XI to Belgian Pilgrims, September 6, 1938

✦

With profound pain the Holy See has learnt that in Slovakia, a country whose virtually total population honors the best Catholic traditions, a "Government Ordinance" has been published . . . which sets down a special "racial legislation" containing various provisions which are in open contrast to Catholic principles.

—Pius XII to Karl Sidor, Slovak Minister to the Holy See, protesting anti-Jewish legislation in Slovakia, November 12, 1941

✦

His Holiness' Secretariat of State trusts that such painful and unjust measures against persons belonging to the Hebrew race cannot be approved by a government which is proud of its Catholic heritage. . . .

> —Pius XII, Second protest to the Slovak government upon learning that fifty-two thousand Slovak Jews were marked for deportation to "labor camps" in Poland, March 14, 1942

✦

The Holy See would . . . neglect its Divine mandate if it would not deplore these enactments and measures which gravely hurt those natural rights of persons merely because of their race. . . .

> —Pius XII, Second protest to the Slovak government upon learning that fifty-two thousand Slovak Jews were marked for deportation to "labor camps" in Poland, March 14, 1942

✦

It is not correct to suppose that deported Jews are sent for labor service; the truth is that they are being annihilated.

> —Pius XII, Second protest to the Slovak government upon learning that fifty-two thousand Slovak Jews were marked for deportation to "labor camps" in Poland, March 14, 1942

✦

We address Your Highness personally, appealing to your noble sentiments in full confidence that you will do everything in your power that so many unfortunate people may be spared other afflictions and other sorrows.

> —Pius XII, Telegram to Admiral Nicholas Horthy, Regent of Hungary, begging him to spare the Jews of Budapest, June 25, 1944

✦

We would like to utter words of fire against such actions; and the only thing restraining us from speaking is the fear of making the plight of the victims worse.

—Pius XII to Archbishop Giovanni Battista Montini (later, Paul VI)

✦

We have been comforted to hear . . . that the Catholics, especially the Catholics in Berlin, have extended much love to the so-called non-Aryans, and in this connection we want to say a special word of fatherly appreciation and heartfelt sympathy for Father Lichtenberg, who is imprisoned.

—Pius XII, on behalf of Monsignor Bernhard Lichtenberg,
Dean of St. Hedwig's Cathedral in Berlin, who was arrested for
denouncing the Nazis' persecution of the Jews.
(Monsignor Lichtenberg died en route to Dachau, 1942.)

✦

Mankind owes that vow [to fight fascism] to the numberless exiles whom the hurricane of war has torn from their native land and scattered in the land of the stranger; who can make their own the lament of the Prophet: "Our inheritance is turned to aliens; our house to strangers." Mankind owes that vow to the hundreds of thousands of persons who, without any fault on their part, sometimes only because of their nationality or race, have been consigned to death or slow extermination.

—Pius XII, Christmas Address, 1942

✦

Above all else comes the saving of human lives.

—Pius XII, to Archbishop Angelo Roncalli (later, John XXIII), 1943

✦

> ## "The mouthpiece of the Jewish war criminals"
>
> {*Following Pius XII's sermon at Christmas, 1942, the Reich Central Security Office prepared a close analysis of the Pope's address for Reinhard Heydrich and submitted it on January 22, 1943.*}
>
> ✦
>
> In a manner never known before, the Pope has repudiated the National Socialist New European Order. His radio allocution was a masterpiece of clerical falsification of the National Socialist *Weltanschauung*. It is true, the Pope does not refer to the National Socialists in Germany by name, but his speech is one long attack on everything we stand for . . . God, he says, regards all peoples and races as worthy of the same consideration. Here he is clearly speaking on behalf of the Jews. . . . That this speech is directed exclusively against the New Order in Europe as seen in National Socialism is clear in the Papal statement that mankind owes a debt to "all who during the war have lost their Fatherland and who, although personally blameless have, simply on account of their nationality and origin, been killed or reduced to utter destitution." Here he is virtually accusing the German people of injustice towards the Jews, and makes himself the mouthpiece of the Jewish war criminals.

We leave it to the [local] bishops to weigh the circumstances in deciding whether or not to exercise restraint, *ad maiora mala vitanda* [to avoid greater evil]. This would be advisable if the danger of retaliatory and coercive measures would be imminent in cases of public statements of the bishop. Here lies one of the reasons we ourselves restrict our public statements. The experience we had in 1942 with documents which we released for distribution to the faithful gives justification, as far as we can see, for our attitude.

—Pius XII, to Konrad von Preysing, Bishop of Berlin, on the murder of Dutch Jews by the Nazis in retaliation for the Catholic bishops of Holland's public condemnation of Nazism's persecution of the Jews, 1943

✦

He who makes a distinction between Jews and other men is unfaithful to God and is in conflict with God's commands.

—Pius XII, Broadcast of Vatican Radio to the people of France, June 1943

✦

Tell your bosses, the Pope is not afraid of concentration camps.

—Pius XII, to a deputy of S. S. Lieutenant Colonel Herbert Kappler, chief of Gestapo forces in Nazi-occupied Rome, 1943

XXXI

THE POPES AND
THE COMMUNISTS

Communism and Catholicism are completely incompatible. Indeed, communism is incompatible with any religion. How could any faith reconcile itself with a philosophy which asserts that there is no God, that the material world is the only reality, and denies that human beings possess an immortal soul?

Yet there is something of a "religious" character to communism. It has a canon of orthodox texts: the writings of Marx, Engels, Lenin—and, in the heyday of *The Little Red Book*, Mao. It has essential doctrines: for example, that the Party can never be in error. It has an eschatology: it looks forward to the coming of an ideal society when all the nations of the world will have submitted to communism. It could even be argued that communism has gods: history, which looks down on the struggling masses as they move toward their inevitable destiny; the Party, the unimpeachable guardian of Communist orthodoxy; and the Communist state, a kind of eternal city in which directing the processes of production always takes precedence over the care of human beings.

Lenin himself said, "The philosophical basis of Marxism is dialectical materialism . . . materialism that is absolutely atheistic, and resolutely opposed to all religion." True to Lenin's teaching, in every nation where it has gained the upper hand, communism has launched a campaign of persecution against religion. Communists claim that while they are "scientific," religion is a sham that deludes the masses. They assert that religion is always an ally of the capitalists, and therefore they oppose it in the name of "justice." Finally, Communists attack religion for the sake of "social progress": by promising an afterlife, they argue, religion urges the masses to accept exploitation and oppression as the natural order of things.

Long before there was a single Communist state, the popes denounced this dangerous philosophy in the strongest terms. It was not long, however, before Communists had an opportunity to put theory into practice. After the Bolshevik Revolution of 1917, the world saw for the first time how Communists would enact their policies of "science, justice, and social progress" in regard to religion.

Before the Revolution, the great mass of the Russian people belonged to the Orthodox Church, yet there was a small Catholic minority. Between 1917 and 1934, the Soviets virtually destroyed the Catholic Church in Russia. All seven archdioceses and dioceses, all two hundred religious houses, all three hundred schools and charitable institutions, the four seminaries and academies, the ten Catholic publishing houses—all were shut down by the Communists. The twenty-one Catholic bishops were imprisoned, deported, or driven into exile. Of the 912 priests and members of religious orders in Russia, by 1934 all but ten were dead, deported, in exile, or had "disappeared." Of the 980 Catholic churches and chapels in the country, only three remained open—one each in Moscow, Leningrad, and Odessa.

The campaign against the Ukrainian Catholics was equally devastating. On April 11 and 12, 1945, agents of the NKVD arrested all the bishops. On April 29, about five hundred priests gathered in the Cathedral of St. George in Lvov to discuss how to face the persecution. While they were in conference, a force of NKVD surrounded the church and opened fire, killing several priests and arresting the survivors. The seminaries were closed and the seminarians were drafted into the Red Army. Then, for ten days, the police occupied the cathedral and the bishop's residence, carrying off religious objects and the entire archives. All the Ukrainian Catholic churches were either closed or handed over to the Orthodox Church.

In Poland, Communists seized the schools and introduced an virulently anti-Christian curriculum. In an effort to alienate the faithful from their priests, Communist newspapers published crude accusations of immorality among the clergy. To further intimidate the laity, priests were arrested in their churches, sometimes even dragged out of the confessional.

The attack on the Church in Poland escalated in 1952. Fifty-nine seminaries were shut down and all the students were sent to labor camps. Approximately one thousand priests were arrested. In 1953, the Communist government ordered the arrest of the Primate, Cardinal Stephen Wyszynski. (He disappeared from sight for two years; the government refused to disclose where the Cardinal was being held.) By the end of 1953, thirty-seven priests had been killed, 260 had disappeared, 350 were deported, seven hundred were in prison, and another seven hundred had gone into exile.

In every nation where the Communists took power, the story was the same.

- *Hungary*. The Primate, Cardinal Joseph Mindszenty, was arrested on December 26, 1948. In prison he was tortured, then given a show trial where he was convicted of treason, espionage, conspiring to overthrow the state, and trading in foreign currency.
- *Lithuania*. Bishop Vincent Borisevicius was arrested in 1946 and sent to a Russian labor camp: he never returned. Bishop Francis

Ramanauskas was deported to Siberia in 1946. Bishop Miecislao Reinys died in a Vladimir prison in 1953.

- *Albania*. Bishop George Sappa was tortured and shot on February 3, 1948. Monsignor Francis Gijni was shot without a trial on March 11, 1948. Archbishop Nicholas Prennhushi was arrested, tortured, and died in prison in August, 1952.
- *Czechoslovakia*. In 1950, two thousand priests and monks were confined in "concentration monasteries" and fifteen hundred nuns were held at "central convents"—each a euphemism for a labor camp. Novices and young religious were drafted into the army. Eventually, ten thousand nuns were expelled from their convents and sentenced to industrial labor.
- *Yugoslavia*. Cardinal Alois Stepinac was sentenced to a labor camp; several hundred nuns were driven out of their convents; the Church of the Redeemer in Fiume was destroyed; crucifixes and other sacred images were profaned throughout the country.
- *Korea*. Missionary priests and nuns were deprived of food-ration cards.
- *Vietnam*. Catholic families were split up and the young people sent to far-off labor camps.

An especially virulent persecution of the Church continues today in the People's Republic of China. When the Communists under Mao Tse-tung took over the country in 1948, they attempted to exterminate the Catholic Church. After several years of violent persecution, the Catholics of China remained steadfast. So the Communists adopted a new tactic. They tried to make the Church in China subservient to the government by creating the Chinese Catholic Patriotic Association, an organization that would be independent of any foreign power (meaning Rome) and come firmly under the control of the Chinese people (meaning the Communist government). To demonstrate the autonomy of the Chinese

Church, foreign missionaries were arrested, publicly humiliated, imprisoned, and finally expelled from the country.

Chinese Catholic priests, religious, and laity who refused to join the Patriotic Association were indicted on a host of absurd charges. Father Joseph Liang, charged with "the crime of celibacy," was tortured to death. Father Charles Chen, charged with "poisoning a well," was shot. Father Thaddeus Wu, charged with "landlordism," was shot. Sister Mary Yao, an Oblate of the Holy Family, was charged with "espionage" and shot. Francis Shen, president of the Legion of Mary, was charged with "secret counterrevolutionary and wicked activities against the government, the people, and Soviet Russia." He was publicly executed.

The Communists described the Bishop of Canton, Dominic Tang Yee-Ming, S.J., as "the most faithful running-dog of the reactionary Vatican." He was imprisoned for twenty-two years, seven years in solitary confinement. He endured endless interrogation sessions. He was starved and denied the most basic necessities. When the shoes he wore at the time of his arrest fell apart, his jailers refused to supply him with another pair. For nearly all of his twenty-two years in jail, Bishop Tang went barefoot. After his release, Archbishop Tang wrote, "When I was a seminarian, I learned to do God's will. God's will required me to practice virtue. . . . There are many opportunities for practicing virtue in prison."

After Father Beda Chang, S.J., the forty-six-year-old rector of St. Ignatius College in Shanghai, was tortured to death in prison, the Party issued a statement denouncing the Masses and prayers that Chinese Catholics were offering for the repose of Father Chang's soul as "a new type of bacteria warfare by the imperialists—a counterrevolutionary mental bacteria."

The darkest day for the Church in Shanghai came on September 8, 1955. The police threw fifteen hundred Catholics in jail.

The seminary was closed. And hundreds of Catholics were required to report daily to their local police station for "re-education" sessions. Foremost among the prisoners of the regime was the Bishop of Shanghai, Ignatius Kung. From the day the Communists took power in China in 1948, Bishop Kung had labored to strengthen the faith of the clergy, religious, and laity for the persecution that would come. After the September 8 mass arrests, Bishop Kung was sentenced to life in prison. He was not released until 1988.

Today, the Patriotic Association is the only "Catholic" organization permitted to operate in China. Chinese Roman Catholics who are in union with the Pope have gone underground to practice their faith. And they suffer ongoing persecution.

November 22, 1995: More than two hundred armed security personnel leveled the Catholic Church in the village of Beidengcun, Qingyuan Province. Fifty villagers were injured in the police action, and seven were arrested.

March 1996: Thirty helicopters and armored cars and five thousand armed troops swept down on pilgrims gathered at China's National Shrine of Our Lady of Dong Lu. They arrested Bishop Su Zhimin, his auxiliary Bishop An Shuxin, and Father Cui Xingang, pastor of the shrine. Then the troops leveled the shrine and confiscated the statue of Our Lady.

April 1996: Layman Wang Chengqun was arrested for donating land to the underground Church. His jailers tortured him so severely that he was left half paralyzed. Rather than have him die in prison, the police sent Wang home.

May 22, 1996: Government security forces looted the underground Catholic Church in Quankuncun, Qungyuan Province, and carried off the Blessed Sacrament.

June–August 1996: Especially crude were the actions taken

against the nuns and priests of Quankuncun. The police abused and humiliated the nuns, then tried to induce them to renounce their vow of chastity. In August, police took several priests and nuns from their prison cells to a dance hall. As dancing girls tried to seduce them, the priests and nuns were photographed. The government publicized the photos in a coarse attempt to destroy the reputation of the priests and nuns.

Spring 1998: The government learned of an orphanage that an elderly underground bishop was operating for eighty physically and mentally handicapped children. The bishop has been warned that if he takes in any more babies, he will be fined $1,250 per child—an astronomical sum in China, where the monthly salary for most villagers is forty dollars.

August 15, 1998: Sister Zhang Yanzhi, an underground Catholic nun, was arrested for teaching catechism to children. A Catholic laywoman, Xie Suqian, who permitted the religion classes to meet in her home, was arrested with Sister Zhang. The children were also punished. They were required to stand, all day, every day, during lessons in the village school.

Most people in the West, even most Catholics, are not aware that the organization passing itself off as the Catholic Church in China is actually the Patriotic Association. Travelers to China find the Catholic Churches open and Sunday Mass celebrated there with great splendor. All of those churches are in the hands of the Patriotic Association. Fortunately, not everyone in the West is mislead. Nina Shea of Freedom House, a human-rights watch group, has gone before congressional committees to explain that "the so-called 'Patriotic Association' [and] its parallel structure known as China Catholic Bishops' College . . . is a pseudo-church controlled totally by the Chinese government."

And certainly Pope John Paul II is able to tell the difference. In an address on December 3, 1996, the Holy Father extolled the underground Catholics of China as "a precious jewel of the Catholic Church." But the Patriotic Association he described as "a church which does not respond either to the will of the Lord Jesus, nor to the Catholic faith."

But the news from China is not all bad. Against all expectations, the Roman Catholic Church there has flourished. In 1948, when the Communists came to power, there were three million Catholics in China. Today there are ten million Catholics faithful to Rome. Even the violence of the Cultural Revolution failed to destroy the Faith.

What Father Peter Paul Heyer, a Divine Word missionary, said almost fifty years ago is still true: "Something supernatural has been planted [in China]. The Communists may be able to drive the visible Church underground, but they can never uproot the Faith."

✦ ✦ ✦

When it is said that the Church is hostile to modern political regimes and that she repudiates the discoveries of modern research, the charge is a ridiculous and groundless calumny. Wild opinions she does repudiate, wicked and seditious projects she does condemn.

—Leo XIII, *Immortale Dei,* November 1, 1885

✦

Let this be understood by all, that the integrity of Catholic faith cannot be reconciled with opinions verging on naturalism or rationalism, the essence of which is utterly to do away with Christian institutions and to install in society the supremacy of man to the exclusion of God.

—Leo XIII, *Immortale Dei,* November 1, 1885

✦

It is a capital evil with respect to the question We are discussing to take for granted that the one class of society is of itself hostile to the other, as if nature had set rich and poor against each other to fight fiercely in implacable war. This is so abhorrent to reason and truth that the exact opposite is true.

—Leo XIII, *Rerum Novarum,* May 15, 1891

✦

Neither capital can do without labor, nor labor without capital.

—Leo XIII, *Rerum Novarum*, May 15, 1891

✦

Communism teaches and seeks two objectives: Unrelenting class warfare and absolute extermination of private ownership. Not secretly or by hidden methods does it do this, but publicly, openly, and by employing every and all means, even the most violent.

—Pius XI, *Quadragesimo Anno,* May 15, 1931

✦

There is nothing which [communism] does not dare, nothing for which it has respect or reverence; and when it has come to power, it is incredible and portentlike in its cruelty and inhumanity.

—Pius XI, *Quadragesimo Anno,* May 15, 1931

✦

The horrible slaughter and destruction through which [Communism] has laid waste vast regions of eastern Europe and Asia are the evidence; how much an enemy and how openly hostile it is to Holy Church and to God Himself is, alas, too well proved by facts and fully known to all.

—Pius XI, *Quadragesimo Anno,* May 15, 1931

✦

Although We, therefore, deem it superfluous to warn upright and faithful children of the Church regarding the impious and iniquitous character of Communism, yet We cannot without deep sorrow contemplate the heedlessness of those who apparently make light of these impending dangers, and with sluggish inertia allow the widespread propagation of doctrine which seeks by violence and slaughter to destroy society altogether.

—Pius XI, *Quadragesimo Anno*, May 15, 1931

✦

All the more gravely to be condemned is the folly of those who neglect to remove or change the conditions that inflame the minds of peoples, and pave the way for the overthrow and destruction of society.

—Pius XI, *Quadragesimo Anno*, May 15, 1931

✦

This Apostolic See, above all, has not refrained from raising its voice, for it knows that its proper and social mission is to defend truth, justice and all those eternal values which Communism ignores or attacks.

—Pius XI, *Divini Redemptoris,* March 19, 1937

✦

The Communism of today, more emphatically than similar movements in the past, conceals in itself a false messianic idea.

—Pius XI, *Divini Redemptoris*, March 19, 1937

✦

A pseudo-ideal of justice, of equality and fraternity in labor impregnates all [Communism's] doctrine and activity with a deceptive

mysticism, which communicates a zealous and contagious enthusiasm to the multitudes entrapped by delusive promises.

—Pius XI, *Divini Redemptoris,* March 19, 1937

✦

Communism, moreover, strips man of his liberty, robs human personality of all its dignity, and removes all the moral restraints that
check the eruptions of blind impulse.

—Pius XI, *Divini Redemptoris,* March 19, 1937

✦

A third powerful factor in the diffusion of Communism is the conspiracy of silence on the part of a large section of the non-Catholic
press of the world. We say conspiracy, because it is impossible otherwise to explain how a press usually so eager to exploit even the little daily incidents of life has been able to remain silent for so long
about the horrors perpetrated in Russia, in Mexico, and even in a
great part of Spain; and that it should have relatively so little to say
concerning a world organization as vast as Russian Communism.

—Pius XI, *Divini Redemptoris,* March 19, 1937

✦

But tear the very idea of God from the hearts of men, and they are
necessarily urged by their passions to the most atrocious barbarity.

—Pius XI, *Divini Redemptoris*, March 19, 1937

✦

Communism is by its nature anti-religious. It considers religion as
"the opiate of the people" because the principles of religion which
speak of a life beyond the grave dissuade the proletariat from the
dream of a Soviet paradise which is of this world.

—Pius XI, *Divini Redemptoris,* March 19, 1937

✦

Communism is intrinsically wrong, and no one who would save Christian civilization may collaborate with it in any undertaking whatsoever.

—Pius XI, *Divini Redemptoris,* March 19, 1937

✦

Those who permit themselves to be deceived into lending their aid towards the triumph of Communism in their own country will be the first to fall victim of their terror.

—Pius XI, *Divini Redemptoris,* March 19, 1937

✦

Those who deliberately and rashly plan to incite the masses to tumult, sedition, or infringement of the liberty of others are certainly not helping to relieve the poverty of the people but are rather increasing it by fomenting mutual hatred.

—Pius XII, *Optatissima Pax,* December 8, 1947

✦

Under an appearance of patriotism, which in reality is just a fraud, this [Chinese Catholic Patriotic Association] aims primarily at making Catholics gradually embrace the tenets of atheistic materialism, by which God Himself is denied and religious principles are rejected.

—Pius XII, *Ad Apostolorum Principis,* June 29, 1958

✦

Man is not just a material organism. He consists also of spirit; he is endowed with reason and freedom. He demands, therefore, a moral and religious order; and it is this order—and not considerations of a purely extraneous, material order which has the greatest validity in the solution of problems relating to his life as an individual and as a member of society, and problems concerning individual states and their inter-relations.

—John XXIII, *Mater et Magistra*, May 15, 1961

✦

The most fundamental modern error is that of imagining that man's natural sense of religion is nothing more than the outcome of feeling or fantasy, to be eradicated from his soul as an anachronism and an obstacle to human progress.

—John XXIII, *Mater et Magistra*, May 15, 1961

✦

And yet this very need for religion reveals a man for what he is: a being created by God and tending always toward God. As we read in St. Augustine: "Lord, you have made us for yourself, and our hearts can find no rest until they rest in you."

—John XXIII, *Mater et Magistra*, May 15, 1961

✦

All social action involves a doctrine. The Christian cannot admit that which is based upon a materialistic and atheistic philosophy, which respects neither the religious orientation of life to its final end, nor human freedom and dignity.

—Paul VI, *Populorum Progressio,* March 26, 1967

✦

The crisis of Marxism does not rid the world of the situations of injustice and oppression which Marxism itself exploited and on which it fed.

—John Paul II, *Centisimus Annus,* May 1, 1991

✦

To those who are searching today for a new and authentic . . . liberation, the Church offers . . . her teaching about the human person redeemed in Christ [and] her concrete commitment and material assistance in the struggle against marginalization and suffering.

—John Paul II, *Centisimus Annus*, May 1, 1991

✦

It should not be forgotten that the whole Church of Slovakia, situated within the communist Republic of Czechoslovakia at the time, suffered painful persecution. Almost all the Bishops were unable to exercise their pastoral service. Many endured cruel imprisonment. Some ended their lives as true martyrs—I am thinking, in particular, of Bishop Wojtassak of the Diocese of Spis, and the Greek Catholic Bishop Pavel Gojdic of Presov. Cardinal Jan Chryzostom Korec, the present Ordinary of Nitra, is a particular witness of this generation of Bishops imprisoned for their faith.

—John Paul II, Slovaks Endured Relentless Persecution, July 5, 1995

✦

The Church in Slovakia has enjoyed religious freedom for only a few years, and perhaps this fact accounts for the great vitality that I could see and feel during my visit.

—John Paul II, Slovaks Endured Relentless Persecution, July 5, 1995

✦

Unity is not the result of human policies or hidden and mysterious intentions. Instead, unity springs from conversion of the heart and from sincere acceptance of the unchanging principles laid down by Christ for his Church.

—John Paul II, Message to Catholics in China, January 14, 1996

✦

"*Disintegrate the underground*"

{*On January 10, 1997, the Donglai Township Committee of the Chinese Communist Party issued a document to local Party functionaries "for legally eradicating the illegal activities of the underground Catholic Church." Excerpts from the statement follow.*}

✦

- "Thoroughly understand all basic characteristics of the vast group of religious believers. . . . Register and set up a file for each one of them."
- "Investigate [the underground Catholic Church], understand its activity schedules, overseas connections, the degree of its stubbornness, the traits that could be taken advantage of, and its psychological characteristics."
- "Induce underground Catholic religious and its core members to carry on their religious activities normally and legally by making them aware of those activities which are in line with theology, those which are unreasonable and illegal . . . indoctrinate them about the policies and objectives of the Party, and the law of the nation."
- "Make a big effort to disintegrate the underground religious influence."

{*The document goes on to suggest methods for "cutting off the relationship between the criminal elements [i.e., underground Catholics] and the overseas enemy force [i.e., the Pope]."*}

continued

- "Prompt the workers to take care of each [underground Catholic], forcing them to write a statement of repentence, to recognize the policy of independence and autonomy, and to join the legal religious activities [of the Catholic Patriotic Association]."
- "If any underground seminary is discovered, it must be categorically eliminated."
- "Firmly eliminate large-scale illegal-assembly activities such as on December 25."
- "Infiltrate the schools. . . . Do not allow students to carry any religious goods or propaganda materials."
- "Disobedience must be punished most severely. Stop firmly the use of religion to interfere with this directive and with other policies such as birth control."

{*To fire up the Party faithful, the document provides a list of "propaganda slogans of the special struggle of eradicating illegal activities in Donglai Township."*}

- "Self administer an independent and autonomous Church!"
- "Actively expand the special struggle of eradicating illegal religious activities in accordance with the laws!"
- "Firmly attack and eradicate the unlawful and criminal activities committed through religion!"
- "Out-of-town religious visitors are not to be allowed!"

Particularly important among these principles is the effective communion of all the parts of the Church with her visible foundation: Peter, the rock. Consequently, a Catholic who wishes to remain such and to be recognized as such cannot reject the principle of communion with the successor of Peter.

—John Paul II, Message to Catholics in China, January 14, 1996

✦

How many testimonies of faith, how many messages of fidelity I have received from communities throughout China! Bishops, priests, religious and lay people have wished to reaffirm their unshakable and full communion with Peter and the rest of the Church.

—John Paul II, Message to Catholics in China, January 14, 1996

✦

Thank God, after the winter of communist domination, a springtime of hope has begun.

—John Paul II, Greeting to Patriarch Teoctist of the Romanian Orthodox Church and President Emil Constantinescu of Romania, May 7, 1999

SOURCES

✦

The Apostolic Fathers, 2nd Ed. translated by J. B. Lightfoot and J. R. Harmer, edited and revised by Michael W. Holmes. Grand Rapids, MI: Baker Book House, 1989.

Baltimore Catechism No. 1, New Revised Ed. Benziger Brothers, Inc., 1961.

The Book of Catholic Quotations, selected and edited by John Chapin. Roman Catholic Books, 1984.

The Book of Saints: A Dictionary of the Servants of God, 6th Ed., compiled by the Benedictine monks of St. Augustine's Abbey. Ramsgate, Morehouse Publishing, 1989.

Calvary and the Mass; A Missal Companion, Archbishop Fulton J. Sheen. P.J. Kenedy & Sons, 1936.

Catechism of the Catholic Church. Libreria Editrice Vaticana, 1994.

Catechism of the "Summa Theologica" of Saint Thomas Aquinas, R. P. Thomas Pegues, O.P. Roman Catholic Books, 1922.

Catholicism, Richard P. McBrien. New York: Harper & Row, 1981.

China's Catholics: Tragedy and Hope in an Emerging Civil Society, Richard Madsen. University of California Press, 1998.

The Christian Faith in the Doctrinal Documents of the Catholic Church, edited by J. Neuner, S.J., and J. Dupuis, S.J. Theological Publications in India, 1973.

Church and Revolution: The Quest for Social Justice in the Catholic Church, Thomas Bokenkotter. New York: Doubleday/Image Books, 1998.

The Conspiracy Against Hitler in the Twilight War, Harold C. Deutsch. Minneapolis, MN: University of Minnesota Press, 1968.

The Correspondence of Pope Gregory VII: Selected Letters from the Registrum, translated by Ephraim Emerton. New York: Octagon Books, 1966.

Creeds, Councils and Controversies: Documents Illustrative of the History of the Church A.D.. *337–461*, edited by J. Stevenson. The Seabury Press, 1966.

The Crisis of Church and State 1050–1300, Brian Tierney. Englewood Cliffs, NJ: Prentice-Hall, 1964.

The Crusades: A Documentary History, translated by James Brundage. Marquette University Press, 1962.

The Development of the Papacy, H. Burn-Murdoch. Faber & Faber Limited, 1954.

The Eucharistic Springtime of the Church, the Most Rev. Richard J. Cushing. St. Paul Editions, 1958.

Fourth Homily on Ecclesiastes, St. Gregory of Nyssa, translated by Richard McCambly. The Gregory of Nyssa Homepage, www.ucc.uconn.edu/~das 93006/nyssa.html.

Gift and Mystery: On the Fiftieth Anniversary of My Priestly Ordination, Pope John Paul II. New York: Doubleday, 1996.

The Gospel of Life [Evangelium Vitae], Pope John Paul II. New York: Times Books, 1995.

The Handbook on Communism, Edited by Joseph M. Bochenski and Gerhart Niemeyer. New York: Frederick A. Praeger, 1962.

The Human Body, selected and arranged by the Monks of Solesmes. St. Paul Editions, 1960.

The Last Three Popes and the Jews, Pinchas E. Lapide. Souvenir Press, 1967.

Latin Hymns, Adrian Fortescue. Roman Catholic Books, 1994.

Making Saints, Kenneth L. Woodward. New York: Simon & Schuster/Touchstone Books, 1996.

The Mass of the Roman Rite: Its Origins and Development, Volumes 1 and II, Joseph A. Jungmann, S.J., translated by Rev. Francis A. Brunner, C.SS.R. Westminster, MD: Christian Classics, Inc., 1986.

The Mission of St. Catherine, Martin Gillet, O.P., translated by Sister M. Thomas Lopez, O.P. B. Herder Book Co., 1946.

The Papal Encyclicals in Their Historical Context, edited by Anne Fremantle. New York: G. P. Putnam's Sons, 1956.

Papal Pronouncements on the Political Order, compiled and edited by Francis J. Powers, C.S.V. The Newman Press, 1952.

Pastoral Care, St. Gregory the Great, translated and annotated by Henry Davis, S.J. The Newman Press, 1950.

Perspectives on the American Catholic Church, 1788–1989, edited by Stephen J. Vicchio and Sister Virginia Geiger. Christian Classics, Inc., 1989.

Pope Honorius Before the Tribunal of Reason and History, Rev. Paul Bottalla, S.J., Burns. Oates & Co., 1868.

The Popes and Slavery, Joel S. Panzer. Staten Island, NY: Alba House, 1996.

Proclaiming Justice & Peace: Papal Documents from *Rerum Novarum* through *Centisimus Annus,* edited by Michael Walsh and Brian Davies. Mystic, CT: Twenty-Third Publications, 1991.

The Red Book of the Persecuted Church, by Albert Galter. The Newman Press, 1957.

The Reform of the Roman Liturgy: Its Problems and Background, Monsignor Klaus Gamber. Una Voce Press/The Foundation for Catholic Reform, 1993.

St. Leo the Great: Letters, translated by Brother Edmund Hunt, C.S.C. Fathers of the Church, Inc., 1957.

St. Nicholas I, Jules Roy, translated by Margaret Maitland. London: Duckworth & Co., 1901.

Saints and Sinners: A History of the Popes, Eamon Duffy. New Haven, CT: Yale University Press, 1997.

The See of Peter, James T. Shotwell and Louise Ropes Loomis. New York: Octagon Books, 1965.

The Silent Church: Facts and Documents Concerning Religious Persecution Behind the Iron Curtain, 2nd Ed. Lino Gussoni. Veritas Publishing Co., Inc., 1957.

Slavery and the Catholic Church, John Francis Maxwell. Barry Rose Publishers, 1975.

Sources of Catholic Dogma, translated by Roy J. Deferrari. B. Herder Book Co., Inc., 1957.

The Vatican in the Age of the Dictators, Anthony Rhodes. New York: Holt, Rinehart and Winston, 1973.

Witness: Writings of Bartolomé de Las Casas, edited and translated by George Sanderlin. Maryknoll, NY: Orbis Books, 1971.